I0012708

Machine Learning

AI Foundations

Machine Learning

AI Foundations

Sergio Ramírez Gallardo

Index

Introduction to Search Algorithms

Definition and Context

Search algorithms are fundamental methods in computing and artificial intelligence. They are used to find solutions to specific problems from a dataset or a state space. In general terms, a search algorithm takes an input, which can be an initial state and a goal, and produces as output a sequence of actions that lead to the desired result.

Imagine that we are in a gigantic library that contains millions of books. If we are looking for a specific book, we need an efficient method to navigate through the numerous shelves and find it. The organization of the library, as well as the strategies and rules we use to search for the book, represent search algorithms in action.

Importance of Search Algorithms in Computing

Search algorithms are crucial in multiple areas, not only in artificial intelligence but also in programming, optimization, and data analysis. Their importance lies in facilitating the resolution of complex problems, optimizing resource use, and improving the efficiency of computing processes.

Resource Optimization

One of the most notable aspects of search algorithms is their ability to optimize resource use. In applications where data can be enormous or where computational resources are limited, having algorithms that search efficiently can save significant time and costs. For example, in cloud computing, where resources are distributed and paid for by use, there are search algorithms that help direct tasks to the most suitable servers, minimizing response time and cost.

Solving Complex Problems

In an increasingly interconnected world, the problems we face are often complex and multidimensional. Search algorithms provide efficient solutions to problems that would otherwise be intractable. For instance, in social networks, friend or content recommendations are a search problem that requires evaluating thousands of connections and data to provide relevant suggestions to users.

Improvement in Efficiency

Additionally, search algorithms improve the efficiency of software applications. In the case of mobile applications, for example, optimized search algorithms can reduce response time in searches, providing a better user experience.

Security and Cybersecurity

Finally, in the realm of cybersecurity, search algorithms are essential for detecting suspicious patterns, evaluating vulnerabilities, and responding to security incidents, making entities more robust against potential threats.

Relationship Between Search Algorithms and Machine Learning

The relationship between search algorithms and machine learning is highly significant, as both fields share several concepts and techniques that allow for efficiently addressing complex problems. In machine learning, search algorithms are used to optimize the models and the solutions derived from them.

A clear example of this relationship is found in hyperparameter search. When training a machine learning model, various hyperparameters often need to be adjusted to achieve optimal performance. Search algorithms, such as grid search or random search, are employed to explore different combinations of these hyperparameters and determine which produces the best model. This optimization process is essential for maximizing accuracy and minimizing error in predictive models.

Furthermore, many machine learning algorithms incorporate search strategies in their internal functioning. For example, algorithms like decision trees or optimization algorithms utilize search techniques to select the most relevant features or to find the best separation between data classes. This emphasizes how machine learning benefits from search methodologies to improve learning efficiency and data interpretation.

Finally, search also plays a critical role in inference tasks in Bayesian models and other machine learning techniques. When evaluating complex models, it is often necessary to perform searches over the parameter space to find those that offer the best explanations for the observed data. This interconnection illustrates how search algorithms and machine learning are not only complementary but also fundamental to advancing the development of effective artificial intelligence technologies.

Applications of Search Algorithms

Search algorithms have a wide range of applications across different fields. Some notable examples include:

- **Games:** In games like chess or checkers, search algorithms are used to evaluate possible moves and determine the best action to take. Algorithms like minimax, for example, evaluate possible moves to minimize the opponent's maximum gain.

- **Robotics:** Robots use search algorithms to find optimal routes in unknown or complex environments. Algorithms like A* allow robots to plan an efficient path in real-time, avoiding obstacles and improving their navigation.

- **Recommendation Systems:** Platforms like Netflix and Amazon use search algorithms to find relevant content for users based on previous behavior patterns. These systems classify and recommend products or movies according to user preferences, enhancing the shopping or viewing experience.

- **Web Search:** Search engines like Google utilize complex algorithms that not only search for keyword matches but also evaluate the relevance of web pages and their standing in relation to others, providing users with more precise and useful results.

- **Fraud Detection:** In financial transaction fraud detection, search algorithms help identify unusual patterns by evaluating large volumes of transactions in real-time. Algorithms like anomaly detection assist in spotting suspicious activity and reducing the risk of fraud.

In summary, search algorithms are essential tools in artificial intelligence and computing in general. From optimization and efficiency to the ability to solve complex problems, their mastery is crucial for addressing contemporary challenges across various disciplines.

Heuristic Search Algorithms

A* Search

A* Search is one of the most commonly used algorithms in artificial intelligence for planning and route finding. Its popularity stems from its ability to find the shortest path from a starting node to a target node in a graph, using a heuristic approach to optimize the search process.

Foundations of A* Search

The A* algorithm combines the properties of uniform cost search and best-first search. It utilizes two key functions to evaluate nodes:

1. **g(n)**: The actual cost of the path from the start node to node n.
2. **h(n)**: A heuristic estimate of the cost from node n to the target, also known as the heuristic function. This component is crucial for the algorithm's performance as it guides the search.

The function f(n) of node n is defined as:

$$f(n) = g(n) + h(n)$$

The A* algorithm selects the node with the lowest f(n) value to explore first. This allows it to efficiently find the shortest path by comparing actual costs and estimates.

Example of A* Search

Imagine we are searching for the shortest route between two cities on a map. The nodes represent the cities, and the edges represent the distances between them. To illustrate how A* works, let's consider the following basic example with cities and their distances:

```
A --(5)--> B
A --(10)--> C
B --(3)--> D
C --(1)--> D
D --(2)--> E
```

We want to find the shortest route from city A to city E. First, we define g(n) and h(n):

- g(A) = 0 (initial cost)
- h(A) = 7 (heuristic estimate of cost from A to E)
- g(B) = 5, h(B) = 4
- g(C) = 10, h(C) = 1
- g(D) = 8, h(D) = 2
- g(E) = 10, h(E) = 0 (target node)

Now, we start the search process:

1. Evaluate A: f(A) = g(A) + h(A) = 0 + 7 = 7.

2. Expand A and evaluate its neighbors B and C:
    - f(B) = g(B) + h(B) = 5 + 4 = 9
    - f(C) = g(C) + h(C) = 10 + 1 = 11
3. Select B (lowest f value) and explore its neighbors:
    - D: f(D) = g(D) = 8 + h(D) = 8 + 2 = 10
4. Expand D and evaluate its neighbor E:
    - E: f(E) = g(E) = 10 + h(E) = 10 + 0 = 10

Since E is our target, and we have found a total cost of 10, the shortest route from A to E is A → B → D → E.

A* Search Implementation in Python

Here is a simple example of how to implement the A* algorithm in Python using a graph represented as a dictionary:

```
import heapq

def a_star(graph, start, goal, heuristics):
    open_set = []
    heapq.heappush(open_set, (0, start))
    came_from = {}
    g_score = {node: float('inf') for node in graph}
    g_score[start] = 0
    f_score = {node: float('inf') for node in graph}
    f_score[start] = heuristics[start]

    while open_set:
        current = heapq.heappop(open_set)[1]

        if current == goal:
```

```
            return reconstruct_path(came_from, current)

        for neighbor, cost in graph[current]:
            tentative_g_score = g_score[current] + cost

            if tentative_g_score < g_score[neighbor]:
                came_from[neighbor] = current
                g_score[neighbor] = tentative_g_score
                f_score[neighbor] = tentative_g_score + heuristics[neighbor]

                if neighbor not in [i[1] for i in open_set]:
                    heapq.heappush(open_set, (f_score[neighbor], neighbor))

    return None

def reconstruct_path(came_from, current):
    total_path = [current]
    while current in came_from:
        current = came_from[current]
        total_path.append(current)
    return total_path[::-1]

# Example graph
graph = {
    'A': [('B', 5), ('C', 10)],
    'B': [('D', 3)],
    'C': [('D', 1)],
    'D': [('E', 2)],
}

heuristics = {
    'A': 7,
```

```
        'B': 4,
        'C': 1,
        'D': 2,
        'E': 0,
}

result = a_star(graph, 'A', 'E', heuristics)
print(f'Shortest path: {result}')
```

In this code, we define a simple graph and a heuristic function. The `a_star` function implements the A* algorithm using a priority queue (implemented by `heapq`) to manage the open nodes. The result is the shortest path from the starting node to the target.

Greedy Search

Greedy Search is another approach used in artificial intelligence that, like A*, employs a heuristic function to decide the next node to explore. However, unlike A*, which considers both accumulated costs and the heuristic, Greedy Search focuses solely on the heuristic function.

Foundations of Greedy Search

In Greedy Search, the algorithm continues to explore the node that appears most promising based on the heuristic without taking into account the total cost of the path to that node. This can lead to quick solutions, but it does not guarantee that the solution is optimal.

Example of Greedy Search

Using the previous example of the cities, let's assume the heuristic function is the same, but now we only utilize h(n) to decide which city to explore:

1. We start at A.
2. The heuristic tells us that C is closer to E (h(C) = 1) compared to B (h(B) = 4).
3. Therefore, we are directed towards C.
4. From C, we can go directly to D, and then from D to E.

However, even though we found a quick path, it is not necessarily the shortest.

Greedy Search Implementation in Python

Below is a simple example in Python that illustrates the implementation of Greedy Search:

```
def greedy_search(graph, start, goal, heuristics):
    open_set = {start}
    came_from = {}
    while open_set:
        current = min(open_set, key=lambda node: heuristics[node])

        if current == goal:
            return reconstruct_path(came_from, current)

        open_set.remove(current)
        for neighbor, cost in graph[current]:
            if neighbor not in came_from:
                came_from[neighbor] = current
                open_set.add(neighbor)

    return None
```

```
greedy_result = greedy_search(graph, 'A', 'E', heuristics)
print(f'Greedy path: {greedy_result}')
```

In this Greedy Search example, we use the heuristic to decide the next node to explore, thereby finding a potentially faster solution, although not necessarily optimal.

Comparison of Heuristic Algorithms

Key Differences

The fundamental difference between A* and Greedy is their approach to node evaluation. A* considers both actual costs and the heuristic, ensuring it finds the optimal solution as long as the heuristic function is admissible and consistent. On the other hand, Greedy Search is faster but does not guarantee finding the shortest path.

Practical Applications

A* is widely used in applications that require an optimal solution, such as navigation systems, video games, and robotics. In contrast, Greedy Search can be useful in situations where finding a quick solution is more crucial than guaranteeing it is the best.

In summary, both heuristic search algorithms have their advantages and disadvantages. The choice between them will depend on the nature of the problem and the application requirements.

Exhaustive Search Algorithms

Brute Force Search

Brute force search is a fundamental technique in problem-solving that involves evaluating all possible solutions to find the best option. This type of search, although inefficient in many cases, is useful in problems where the solution space is small or when more optimized approaches do not exist.

Fundamentals of Brute Force Search

The brute force technique involves exhaustively exploring all possible combinations of solutions for a given problem. Let's imagine a simple example: if we are looking for the correct combination of a 4-digit lock, we would have to try all possible combinations from 0000 to 9999, which means 10,000 combinations.

This extends to more complex problems, such as solving puzzles, finding paths in graphs, or performing optimizations. The advantage of brute force search is its simplicity and guaranteed ability to find the optimal solution in problems where conditions permit.

Example of Brute Force Search

Consider a classic problem: the Knapsack Problem. Suppose we have a knapsack that can carry a maximum weight of 10 kg and several items, each with an associated weight and value. The goal is to maximize the total value of the items we can carry in the knapsack.

The steps for a brute force search would be:

1. List all items and their respective combinations.
2. Calculate the total weight and value for each combination.
3. Select the combination that does not exceed the weight limit and has the highest value.

Imagine we have the following items:

- Item 1: Weight = 5 kg, Value = 10
- Item 2: Weight = 3 kg, Value = 7
- Item 3: Weight = 4 kg, Value = 6

The possible combinations that do not exceed the weight of 10 kg are:

1. Item 1
2. Item 2
3. Item 3
4. Item 1 + Item 2
5. Item 1 + Item 3

6. Item 2 + Item 3
7. Item 1 + Item 2 + Item 3

Evaluating each combination, we find their corresponding values and weights. The best combination that maximizes the value without exceeding 10 kg is Item 1 + Item 2, resulting in a total value of 17.

Implementation of Brute Force Search in Python

Below is an example of implementing brute force search for the Knapsack Problem:

```python
from itertools import combinations

def brute_force_knapsack(weights, values, capacity):
    num_elements = len(weights)
    best_value = 0
    best_combination = []

    # Generate all possible combinations
    for r in range(num_elements + 1):
        for combination in combinations(range(num_elements), r):
            total_weight = sum(weights[i] for i in combination)
            total_value = sum(values[i] for i in combination)

            if total_weight <= capacity and total_value > best_value:
                best_value = total_value
                best_combination = combination

    return best_combination, best_value
```

```
weights = [5, 3, 4]
values = [10, 7, 6]
capacity = 10

combination, value = brute_force_knapsack(weights, values, capacity)
print(f'Best combination: {combination}, Total value: {value}')
```

In this code, we use the `itertools` library to generate all possible combinations of items. The `brute_force_knapsack` function iterates through each combination and calculates its total weight and value, updating the best option as it finds combinations that maximize the value without exceeding the capacity.

Backtracking: Fundamentals and Applications

Backtracking is a more sophisticated technique than brute force search. It is based on the idea of incrementally building solutions, testing each option, and backtracking when a solution is found to be invalid. This technique is particularly effective in problems where the solution space is significant, but combinations that do not meet certain criteria can be quickly discarded.

How Does Backtracking Work?

Imagine we are solving a Sudoku puzzle. The backtracking algorithm starts in an empty cell and tries a number. If the number is valid, it is placed in the cell, and the algorithm proceeds to the next empty cell. If at any point the algorithm finds that there are no valid numbers for a cell, it will backtrack to the previous cell, change the tested number, and continue its search.

This technique is very powerful because it avoids exploring combinations that cannot lead to a valid solution. Instead of testing all possible combinations, it only explores those that seem promising.

Example of Backtracking

Consider the N-Queens problem, where the goal is to place N queens on a chessboard in such a way that no two queens threaten each other. Using backtracking, we can start by placing a queen in the first row and then try to place a queen in the second row, ensuring it is not threatened by the first. If a placement proves invalid, we backtrack and try the next option.

Implementation of Backtracking in Python

Below is an example of how to implement the backtracking algorithm for the N-Queens problem:

```
def is_safe(board, row, col, N):
    # Check the column
    for i in range(row):
        if board[i][col] == 'Q':
            return False
    # Check the upper left diagonal
    for i, j in zip(range(row, -1, -1), range(col, -1, -1)):
        if board[i][j] == 'Q':
            return False
    # Check the upper right diagonal
    for i, j in zip(range(row, -1, -1), range(col, N)):
        if board[i][j] == 'Q':
            return False
```

```
    return True

def solve_n_queens(board, row, N):
    if row >= N:
        return True
    for col in range(N):
        if is_safe(board, row, col, N):
            board[row][col] = 'Q'
            if solve_n_queens(board, row + 1, N):
                return True
            board[row][col] = '.'  # Backtrack
    return False

def display_board(board):
    for row in board:
        print(' '.join(row))

N = 4
board = [['.' for _ in range(N)] for _ in range(N)]
if solve_n_queens(board, 0, N):
    display_board(board)
else:
    print("No solution.")
```

In this code, the `solve_n_queens` function attempts to place queens row by row. The `is_safe` function ensures that the current placement is valid. If a queen cannot be placed in a row, it backtracks and tests the next column.

Backtracking in Combination and Permutation Problems

Backtracking is also widely used in combination and permutation problems. For example, in the letter combination problem, we can use backtracking to generate all possible combinations of a word. The approach would be to keep adding letters to the combination until the desired length is reached, backtracking when no further progress can be made.

In summary, brute force search and backtracking are fundamental in the field of artificial intelligence for solving complex problems. The choice between both methods depends on the type of problem to be solved and the specific constraints at hand. Brute force search can be useful for small and manageable solution spaces, while backtracking allows for optimized searches in larger and more complex problems, avoiding unnecessary evaluations.

Local Search Algorithms

Definition and Principles of Local Search

Local search is an optimization technique used to solve problems where an optimal solution must be found from a given search space. Unlike exhaustive techniques that evaluate all possible solutions, local search focuses on exploring a subset of solutions in a neighborhood. This strategy is highly efficient and is often applied in problems where the solution space is too large to address exhaustively.

The essence of local search lies in starting with an initial solution and then iterating to improve it through locally optimal moves, typically based on small changes to the current solution. A fundamental aspect of local search is the notion of "neighborhood," which defines which solutions are considered accessible from the current solution.

Gradient Descent Algorithms

One of the most well-known methods within local search is the gradient descent algorithm. This algorithm is primarily used in continuous optimization problems, where the goal is to minimize a cost function.

Fundamentals of Gradient Descent

Gradient descent operates by moving in the opposite direction of the gradient of the function to be minimized. In simple terms, the gradient points in the direction where the function increases the fastest. Therefore, moving in the opposite direction means moving towards the optimal solution.

Imagine a mountainous landscape where the goal is to find the lowest point (the optimal solution). Gradient descent begins at any point on the landscape and calculates the slope. Then it moves in the steepest downward direction, repeating this process until it reaches the bottom of the valley.

Example of Gradient Descent

Suppose we want to minimize a simple quadratic function, such as $f(x) = (x-3)^2$. The global minimum of this function is $x = 3$.

The implementation of gradient descent in this case would involve:

1. Choosing an initial point, for example $x_0 = 0$.
2. Calculating the derivative of the function, which in this case is $f'(x) = 2(x-3)$.
3. Updating the value of x by subtracting a fraction of the gradient:

$$x_{new} = x_{old} - \eta \cdot f'(x_{old})$$

where η is the learning rate.

We develop an example in Python:

```
def quadratic_function(x):
    return (x - 3) ** 2

def derivative(x):
    return 2 * (x - 3)

def gradient_descent(initial_x, learning_rate,
 num_iterations):
    x = initial_x
    for _ in range(num_iterations):
        x = x - learning_rate * derivative(x)
    return x

initial_x = 0
learning_rate = 0.1
num_iterations = 100

result = gradient_descent(initial_x, learning_rate,
 num_iterations)
print(f'The optimal value found is: {result}')
```

In this code, we define the quadratic function and its derivative. The `gradient_descent` function takes the initial point, the learning rate, and the number of iterations to progressively improve the solution until it converges towards the minimum.

Challenges of Gradient Descent

While gradient descent is a powerful method, it presents certain challenges, such as:

- **Getting Stuck in Local Minima:** The algorithm may converge to a local minimum rather than reaching the global minimum. This is common in non-convex functions.
- **Choice of Learning Rate:** A learning rate that is too high can result in excessive jumps, preventing the algorithm from converging, while a rate that is too low may lead to very slow convergence.
- **Heterogeneity of the Search Space:** In search spaces with many peaks and valleys, gradient descent can be ineffective.

Simulated Annealing

Simulated Annealing is another local search algorithm that seeks to approximate the optimal solution. It is inspired by the physical process of cooling metal to settle into the lowest energy state possible.

Fundamentals of Simulated Annealing

Unlike gradient descent, which always seeks to improve the solution, Simulated Annealing allows movements to worse solutions with a controlled probability. This approach is fundamental to avoid getting trapped in a local minimum.

This algorithm begins with a high temperature, allowing for free exploration of the solution space. As the search progresses, the temperature is reduced, limiting the opportunities to accept changes towards worse solutions and moving towards exploiting the solutions found.

Example of Simulated Annealing

Suppose we again want to minimize the quadratic function $f(x) = (x - 3)^2$. The Simulated Annealing process would consist of:

1. Starting with a random x (high temperature).
2. Testing movements in the neighborhood. If the new x reduces the cost function, it is accepted. If it increases, it is accepted with a probability based on the temperature.
3. Reducing the temperature over time and repeating until the optimal solution is found or a stopping criterion is reached.

We implement Simulated Annealing in Python:

```
import random
import math

def simulated_annealing(initial_x, initial_temp, final_temp, alpha, num_iterations):
    current_x = initial_x
    best_x = current_x
    best_cost = quadratic_function(current_x)

    temperature = initial_temp

    while temperature > final_temp:
        for _ in range(num_iterations):
            new_x = current_x + random.uniform(-1, 1)  # Random movement in the neighborhood
            current_cost = quadratic_function(current_x)
            new_cost = quadratic_function(new_x)
```

```
            # If the new cost is better or it is accepted with probability
            if new_cost < current_cost or random.uniform(0, 1) < math.exp((current_cost - new_cost) / temperature):
                current_x = new_x

            # Update the best solution
            if new_cost < best_cost:
                best_cost = new_cost
                best_x = new_x

        # Reduce the temperature
        temperature *= alpha

    return best_x

initial_x = random.uniform(-10, 10)
initial_temp = 1000
final_temp = 1
alpha = 0.95
num_iterations = 100

result = simulated_annealing(initial_x, initial_temp, final_temp, alpha, num_iterations)
print(f'The optimal value found is: {result}')
```

In this code, the algorithm starts exploring from a random value and allows movements towards better or worse solutions depending on the temperature. The controlled reduction of temperature allows the algorithm to stabilize on optimal solutions as it progresses.

Advantages and Disadvantages of Simulated Annealing

- **Advantages:**
    - Ability to escape local minima.
    - Flexibility in exploring the search space.
- **Disadvantages:**
    - The choice of parameters such as cooling rate is crucial.
    - It may require more computation time compared to simpler local search methods.

Genetic Algorithms

Genetic algorithms today represent a different but related approach to local search. Based on the principles of natural evolution, these algorithms explore the solution space by simulating the processes of natural selection and genetics.

Fundamentals of Genetic Algorithms

A genetic algorithm begins with an initial population of possible solutions (individuals) and applies evolutionary operators such as selection, crossover, and mutation. Through cycles of selection and evaluation, the population evolves, improving over time.

Imagine that we are trying to optimize a function that seeks to maximize the area of a rectangle. An initial population of rectangles (each defined by its width and height) undergoes multiple generations of evolution to find the optimal shape.

Example of Genetic Algorithms

Consider the following scheme to optimize the area function $A = width \times height$:

1. Generate an initial population of rectangles.
2. Evaluate the objective function (area).
3. Select individuals based on their fitness (area).
4. Perform crossover to combine features of the parents.
5. Mutate some individuals to maintain genetic diversity.
6. Repeat until a number of generations is reached or an optimal solution is found.

Here is an outline in Python that illustrates a genetic algorithm:

```
import random

def evaluation(individual):
    width, height = individual
    return width * height  # Area of the rectangle

def selection(population):
    return max(population, key=evaluation)  # Selects the best individual

def crossover(parent1, parent2):
    return (
        (parent1[0] + parent2[0]) / 2,
        (parent1[1] + parent2[1]) / 2
```

```
    )

def mutation(individual, mutation_rate):
    if random.random() < mutation_rate:
        return (individual[0] + random.uniform(-1, 1), individual[1] + random.uniform(-1, 1))
    return individual

def genetic_algorithm(population_size, generations, mutation_rate):
    population = [(random.uniform(1, 10), random.uniform(1, 10)) for _ in range(population_size)]

    for _ in range(generations):
        best_individual = selection(population)
        new_population = []

        for _ in range(population_size // 2): # Create new population
            parent1 = best_individual  # Select the best
            parent2 = selection(population) # Select another
            child = crossover(parent1, parent2)
            mutated_child = mutation(child, mutation_rate)
            new_population.append(mutated_child)

        population = new_population

    return selection(population)

population_size = 10
generations = 100
mutation_rate = 0.1

result = genetic_algorithm(population_size, generations,
```

```
    mutation_rate)
print(f'The best rectangle found has area: {evaluation(
result)} with dimensions: {result}')
```

In this code, we start by creating an initial population of rectangles, evaluate their area as an objective function, and throughout the generations evolve the individuals using crossover and mutations.

Advantages and Disadvantages of Genetic Algorithms

- **Advantages:**
    - Effective in large spaces.
    - Versatility to be applied across a wide variety of problems.
- **Disadvantages:**
    - Require careful parameter selection like mutation rate and population size.
    - Can be computationally expensive.

Conclusion

Local search is an invaluable strategy in solving complex problems in artificial intelligence and optimization. From gradient descent, which seeks to adjust solutions based on the slope of a function, to methods like Simulated Annealing and Genetic Algorithms that allow for innovative exploration of the search space, each approach has its strengths and challenges. The choice of the appropriate method will depend on the nature of the problem in question and the characteristics of the search space to be explored. The importance of understanding and applying these techniques lies not only in solving current problems but also in paving the way for new solutions and future developments in the field of artificial intelligence.

Introduction to Machine Learning

Definition and Context

Machine learning is a branch of artificial intelligence that allows systems to learn and improve automatically from experience without being explicitly programmed. Essentially, instead of being programmed to perform specific tasks, machine learning systems use data to identify patterns and make predictions or decisions based on those patterns.

Imagine a child learning to recognize animals. Instead of telling them what a dog or a cat is using specific rules, you show them many images of different animals and tell them which are dogs and which are cats. Over time, the child starts to identify characteristics that differentiate dogs from cats and can make predictions about new animals they have never seen before. This is the principle behind machine learning.

The capability of a system to learn from data and improve its performance over time has become fundamental in today's world, where the amount of available information is constantly growing.

History and Evolution of Machine Learning

The concept of machine learning is not new; it has its roots in the 1950s. However, it has significantly evolved over the last few decades due to technological advances, the growth of data storage capacity, and the processing power of computers.

The Early Years

The term "machine learning" was coined by Arthur Samuel in 1959. Samuel developed a computer program that played checkers and learned from its own experiences. This system could adapt and improve its playing ability over time, laying the foundations for modern machine learning.

In the following decades, various algorithms and techniques were developed, from the perceptron, the precursor to neural networks, to the early classification algorithms like the k-nearest neighbors (k-NN) algorithm. However, progress was limited due to computational constraints and a scarcity of data.

The Renaissance of Machine Learning

The shift came in the 2000s when a renaissance in machine learning took place. This renaissance was driven by several factors:

1. **Big Data:** The explosion of data generated by the internet, mobile devices, and sensors has provided a valuable resource for training machine learning models.

2. **Computational Power:** Advances in hardware, such as the use of graphics processing units (GPUs) and cloud computing technologies, have enabled the handling of large datasets and performing complex computations efficiently.

3. **Advancements in Algorithms:** New techniques, such as deep learning, have allowed for the construction of more complex and accurate models that surpass the capabilities of classical algorithms.

Today, machine learning is applied in various fields, from medicine to finance, e-commerce, and industrial automation.

Types of Learning (Supervised, Unsupervised, Semi-Supervised)

Machine learning can be classified into several categories, the most common being supervised learning, unsupervised learning, and semi-supervised learning. Each has distinct characteristics and is applied to different types of problems.

Supervised Learning

In supervised learning, the model is trained using a labeled dataset. This means that the input data is accompanied by the expected output, allowing the model to learn to make predictions based on new inputs.

Example: Email Classification

Imagine a system that must classify emails as "spam" or "not spam." To train the model, a set of previously labeled emails as spam or not spam is needed. As the model is trained, it adjusts its parameters to predict the correct category for unlabeled emails.

The algorithms used in supervised learning include:

- **Linear Regression:** For continuous prediction problems.
- **Decision Trees:** Which split the data into subgroups based on features.
- **Support Vector Machines (SVM):** Which seek to find the best separating boundary between classes.

Unsupervised Learning

In unsupervised learning, the model is trained using an unlabeled dataset, meaning that the system must find patterns and relationships in the data on its own.

Example: Customer Segmentation

Suppose we have a dataset of customer transactions at a store. An unsupervised learning model can cluster customers into segments based on their purchasing behavior without needing prior information about customer categories.

The algorithms used in unsupervised learning include:

- **K-Means Clustering:** Which divides the data into k groups based on similarity.
- **Principal Component Analysis (PCA):** Which reduces the dimensionality of the data while preserving variability.

Semi-Supervised Learning

Semi-supervised learning combines elements of supervised and unsupervised learning. A small labeled dataset is used alongside a larger unlabeled dataset. This is useful in situations where labeling all the data is costly or time-consuming.

Example: Image Labeling

Imagine a set of images where only a small number of them are labeled. A model can learn from the labeled images and then apply that learning to classify the unlabeled images.

Semi-supervised learning is useful when one wants to increase the model's accuracy without investing significant resources in labeling large volumes of data.

Applications of Machine Learning

Machine learning has become an invaluable tool across a wide variety of industries. Some examples of its applications include:

1. **Medicine:** Diagnosing diseases from medical images, analyzing genomic data, and predicting disease outbreaks.
2. **Finance:** Credit risk analysis, fraud detection, and market trend prediction.
3. **E-Commerce:** Personalized recommendations for customers, price optimization, and sentiment analysis of product reviews.
4. **Transportation:** Route optimization for logistics and GPS navigation, as well as traffic predictions.
5. **Entertainment:** Recommendation systems on streaming platforms like Netflix and Spotify, suggesting content based on user preferences.

In summary, machine learning not only transforms the way we interact with technology but also offers innovative solutions to complex problems across numerous sectors. As techniques continue to evolve and the availability of data continues to increase, the opportunities to apply machine learning are nearly limitless.

Fundamentals of Regression

Concept of Regression

Regression is a statistical technique used to model and analyze the relationship between a dependent variable (or response) and one or more independent variables (or predictors). Its main objective is to predict the value of the dependent variable based on the values of the independent variables. This process becomes a powerful tool in both scientific research and business decision-making.

To illustrate this concept, imagine that we want to predict the price of a home. In this context, the price of the home is the dependent variable, while characteristics such as size, location, number of rooms, and age of the home are independent variables. Through regression, we can establish a relationship between these variables that allows us to predict the price of a home based on its characteristics.

Simple Linear Regression

Simple linear regression is the most basic case of regression, where a linear relationship is established between a dependent variable and a single independent variable. Mathematically, the relationship can be represented as:

$Y = \beta_0 + \beta_1 X +$ �

Where:

- Y is the dependent variable.
- β_0 is the intercept (the value of Y when $X = 0$).
- β_1 is the slope of the line (the change in Y for each unit change in X).
- X is the independent variable.
- � is the error term, which captures the variability in Y that is not explained by X.

Example of Simple Linear Regression

Let's suppose we have data on the number of hours a group of students studies and their respective grades on an exam. We want to predict a student's grade based on how many hours they study. The data may look like this:

Study Hours (X)	Grade (Y)
1	60
2	65
3	70

Study Hours (X)	Grade (Y)
4	75
5	80

If we plot these points, we will see that they roughly form a straight line. Simple linear regression will find the best line that minimizes the sum of squared errors (the vertical distance from each point to the line).

To carry out this analysis in Python, we can use the `statsmodels` library as follows:

```
import numpy as np
import pandas as pd
import statsmodels.api as sm
import matplotlib.pyplot as plt

# Sample Data
data = {
    'Study Hours': [1, 2, 3, 4, 5],
    'Grade': [60, 65, 70, 75, 80]
}

df = pd.DataFrame(data)

# Define independent and dependent variables
X = df['Study Hours']
y = df['Grade']

# Add a constant to the independent variable
X = sm.add_constant(X)

# Fit the linear regression model
model = sm.OLS(y, X).fit()

# Model summary
```

```python
print(model.summary())

# Plot the data and regression line
plt.scatter(df['Study Hours'], df['Grade'], color='blue', label='Data')
plt.plot(df['Study Hours'], model.predict(X), color='red', label='Regression Line')
plt.xlabel('Study Hours')
plt.ylabel('Grade')
plt.legend()
plt.title('Simple Linear Regression')
plt.show()
```

In this example, after running the analysis, the model will provide estimates for β_0 and β_1 and a series of statistics that help evaluate the quality of the model, such as the R^2 value, which indicates the proportion of variation in Y that is explained by X.

Multiple Linear Regression

Multiple linear regression expands to situations where a dependent variable is related to multiple independent variables. The relationship is expressed as:

$$Y = \beta_0 + \beta_1 X_1 + \beta_2 X_2 + \ldots + \beta_n X_n +$$ �

Where $X_1, X_2, \ldots, X_n$ are the independent variables.

Example of Multiple Linear Regression

Suppose we want to predict the price of a home based on several characteristics: size (in square meters), number of rooms, and age of the house. The data may be:

Size (X1)	Rooms (X2)	Age (X3)	Price (Y)
50	2	10	150000
60	3	5	200000
80	3	2	250000
100	4	1	300000
120	5	0	350000

To apply multiple linear regression in Python, we can use the following code:

```
# Sample Data
data = {
    'Size': [50, 60, 80, 100, 120],
    'Rooms': [2, 3, 3, 4, 5],
    'Age': [10, 5, 2, 1, 0],
    'Price': [150000, 200000, 250000, 300000, 350000]
}

df = pd.DataFrame(data)

# Define independent and dependent variables
X = df[['Size', 'Rooms', 'Age']]
y = df['Price']

# Add a constant to the independent variables
X = sm.add_constant(X)

# Fit the linear regression model
multiple_model = sm.OLS(y, X).fit()

# Model summary
print(multiple_model.summary())
```

By running this code, we will obtain the coefficients for each independent variable, allowing us to interpret how each one affects the price of the home. For example, it is possible that the size of the house has a more significant impact on its price than the age of the house.

Model Validation and Adjustment

Validating and adjusting a regression model are essential steps to ensure that the model is reliable and usable for prediction. Without an adequate validation process, there is a risk that the model overfits the training data and does not generalize well to new data.

Splitting the Dataset

A common practice for validating a regression model is to split the dataset into a training set and a test set. This allows us to fit the model using the training set and then evaluate its performance on the test set, which was not used during fitting. A typical approach is to use 70% of the dataset for training and 30% for testing.

To do this in Python, you can use:

```
from sklearn.model_selection import train_test_split

# Split the data into training and testing sets
X_train, X_test, y_train, y_test = train_test_split(X, y,
    test_size=0.3, random_state=42)
```

Evaluating Model Performance

Several metrics are used to evaluate the performance of the regression model. Some of the most common are:

- **R^2 (Coefficient of Determination):** Indicates the proportion of variability in the dependent variable that is explained by the independent variables. An R^2 value close to 1 indicates that the model explains a large proportion of the variability. It is calculated as:

$$R^2 = 1 - \frac{SS_{res}}{SS_{tot}}$$

where SS_{res} is the sum of squared residuals and SS_{tot} is the total sum of squares.

- **Mean Squared Error (MSE):** Measures the average of the squared errors between the predicted values and the actual values. It is calculated as:

$$MSE = \frac{1}{n} \sum_{i=1}^{n} (y_i - \hat{y}_i)^2$$

where n is the total number of observations, y_i is the true value, and $\hat{y}_i$ is the predicted value.

- **Root Mean Squared Error (RMSE):** Is the square root of the MSE and is expressed in the same units as the dependent variable, making its interpretation easier. It is calculated as:

$$RMSE = \sqrt{MSE}$$

These metrics can be calculated in Python using the `sklearn` library:

```
from sklearn.metrics import mean_squared_error, r2_score

# Fit the model with the training set
final_model = sm.OLS(y_train, sm.add_constant(X_train)).fit()

# Make predictions on the testing set
y_pred = final_model.predict(sm.add_constant(X_test))
```

```
# Calculate metrics
mse = mean_squared_error(y_test, y_pred)
r2 = r2_score(y_test, y_pred)

print(f'Mean Squared Error: {mse}')
print(f'R²: {r2}')
```

The results of these metrics provide a clear idea of how the model performs on unseen data, allowing us to assess whether it has learned adequately from the training data.

Hyperparameter Tuning

Hyperparameter tuning is the process of optimizing certain parameters of the model to improve its performance. In the context of regression, this tuning can be done through regularization, a technique that helps prevent overfitting by adding a penalty term to the loss function.

Several common regularization techniques exist:

- **Ridge Regression (L2 Regularization):** Adds a penalty to the square of the coefficients. This means that the larger the coefficients, the greater the penalty. It is useful when many predictors are suspected to have an impact on the response.

  In Python, it can be implemented as follows:

  ```
  from sklearn.linear_model import Ridge

  ridge_model = Ridge(alpha=1.0)
  ridge_model.fit(X_train, y_train)
  ```

- **Lasso Regression (L1 Regularization):** Adds a penalty to the sum of the absolute values of the coefficients. This has the effect of eliminating some predictors, as it forces their coefficients to be exactly zero, which is useful for feature selection.

Here is an example in Python:

```
from sklearn.linear_model import Lasso

lasso_model = Lasso(alpha=0.1)
lasso_model.fit(X_train, y_train)
```

- **Elastic Net:** Combines both L1 and L2 regularizations and is useful when there are correlations among the predictors.

```
from sklearn.linear_model import ElasticNet

en_model = ElasticNet(alpha=1.0, l1_ratio=0.5)
en_model.fit(X_train, y_train)
```

It is important to perform proper hyperparameter search to find the optimal values. This can be done using techniques like cross-validation, where the training set is divided into multiple folds, ensuring that the model is evaluated on different subsets of the data.

```
from sklearn.model_selection import GridSearchCV

# Define the range of hyperparameters for Ridge
param_grid = {'alpha': [0.1, 1.0, 10.0]}

ridge_cv = GridSearchCV(Ridge(), param_grid, cv=5)
ridge_cv.fit(X_train, y_train)

print(f'Best hyperparameter for Ridge: {ridge_cv.best_params_
  }')
```

Using `GridSearchCV` allows for systematic exploration of various parameter combinations and choosing the best option.

Conclusion

The fundamentals of regression form an essential foundation in machine learning and statistics. Whether we are working with simple or multiple linear regression, it is crucial to understand how relationships between variables are modeled and how reliable predictions can be made. Model evaluation, validation, and hyperparameter tuning are critical steps in ensuring a robust and effective model. By correctly applying these techniques, valuable insights can be gained that inform decisions across a variety of contexts, from scientific research to industry. Regression not only provides tools to understand the past but also offers a clear vision toward the future, enabling better data-driven decision-making.

Advanced Regression Techniques

Logistic Regression

Logistic regression is a statistical analysis technique used to model the probability of an event, particularly when the dependent variable is categorical. It is commonly used in binary classification problems, where the output can take one of two values, such as "yes" or "no," "fraud" or "no fraud."

Fundamentals of Logistic Regression

Unlike linear regression, which seeks to fit a straight line to the data, logistic regression aims to find a function that predicts the probability of the event occurring. This probability is calculated using the logistic function, also known as the sigmoid function, which has the following form:

$$P(Y=1 \mid X) = \frac{1}{1+e^{-(\beta_0+\beta_1 X_1+\beta_2 X_2+...+\beta_n X_n)}}$$

Where:

- $P(Y=1 \mid X)$ represents the probability that the dependent variable Y takes the value 1 given n independent variables $X_1, X_2, ..., X_n$.
- e is the base of the natural logarithm.
- $\beta_0, \beta_1, ..., \beta_n$ are the coefficients that are adjusted during the training process.

The logistic function transforms any real value into the range of 0 to 1, allowing for interpretation of the results as probabilities.

Example of Logistic Regression

Imagine a scenario where we want to predict whether a student will pass an exam based on the number of hours studied and the grade point average. Let's define our variables:

- Y: dependent variable (1 if passing, 0 if not).
- X_1: hours studied.
- X_2: grade point average.

Assume we have the following data:

Hours Studied (X1)	Grade Point Average (X2)	Pass (Y)
1	60	0
2	65	0
3	70	1
4	75	1
5	85	1

We can use logistic regression to fit a model to this information and predict whether a new student, who studied for 3 hours and has a GPA of 68, will pass the exam.

To implement this in Python, we can use the `statsmodels` library. The following code illustrates how to fit a logistic regression model:

```
import pandas as pd
import statsmodels.api as sm

# Example data
data = {
    'Hours Studied': [1, 2, 3, 4, 5],
    'Grade Point Average': [60, 65, 70, 75, 85],
    'Pass': [0, 0, 1, 1, 1]
}

df = pd.DataFrame(data)

# Define independent and dependent variables
X = df[['Hours Studied', 'Grade Point Average']]
y = df['Pass']

# Add a constant to the independent variables
X = sm.add_constant(X)

# Fit the logistic regression model
logistic_model = sm.Logit(y, X)
result = logistic_model.fit()

# Model summary
print(result.summary())

# Prediction for a new student
new_student = pd.DataFrame({'const': 1, 'Hours Studied': [3
```

```
    ], 'Grade Point Average': [68]})
probability = result.predict(new_student)
print(f'Probability of passing: {probability[0]}')
```

This model will provide the coefficients for each independent variable and allow predicting the probability that the new student will pass the exam.

Interpretation of Coefficients in Logistic Regression

Once a logistic regression model has been fitted, it is important to interpret the coefficients. The interpretation is not as straightforward as in linear regression. For each coefficient β_i, the **odds ratio** can be calculated:

$$\text{Odds Ratio} = e^{\beta_i}$$

The odds ratio represents the odds of success for a one-unit change in the independent variable. For example, if the coefficient for "Hours Studied" is 0.5, then the odds ratio is $e^{0.5} \approx 1.65$, indicating that each additional hour of study increases the odds of passing by 65%.

Evaluation of Logistic Regression Models

It is essential to evaluate the performance of a logistic regression model to ensure it is effective and generalizes well to new data. Some metrics and techniques for this are:

Confusion Matrix

The confusion matrix allows for visualizing the performance of the model by providing a summary of the predictions made. It is organized in a table format that shows the number of true positives, true negatives, false positives, and false negatives.

Precision, Recall, and F1-Score

Precision, recall, and F1-score metrics are useful for assessing the effectiveness of a classification model.

- **Precision:** The proportion of true positives to the total predicted positives.

$$\text{Precision} = \frac{\text{TP}}{\text{TP+FP}}$$

- **Recall:** The proportion of true positives to the total actual positives.

$$\text{Recall} = \frac{\text{TP}}{\text{TP+FN}}$$

- **F1-Score:** The harmonic mean of precision and recall, which helps to balance both metrics.

$$\text{F1-Score} = 2 \cdot \frac{\text{Precision} \cdot \text{Recall}}{\text{Precision+Recall}}$$

To calculate these metrics and create the confusion matrix in Python, the `sklearn` module can be used:

```
from sklearn.metrics import confusion_matrix, accuracy_score,
    classification_report

# Predictions on the test set
y_pred = (result.predict(X) > 0.5).astype(int)

# Calculate the confusion matrix
cm = confusion_matrix(y, y_pred)
print(f'Confusion Matrix:\n{cm}')

```

```
# Calculate precision and recall
precision = accuracy_score(y, y_pred)
print(f'Precision: {precision}')

# Complete report
print(classification_report(y, y_pred))
```

Evaluation of Regression Models

In addition to classification-specific metrics, cross-validation techniques are needed to evaluate the model's generalization capability. Cross-validation involves splitting the dataset into several subsets, training the model multiple times, and averaging the performance metrics.

Regularization in Logistic Regression

Regularization is a technique used to prevent overfitting in logistic regression models, especially when there are a large number of predictors. Two common forms of regularization are:

- **Ridge Regression (L2):** Adds a penalty equal to the square of the magnitude of the coefficients. This helps to reduce variability without eliminating features.
- **Lasso Regression (L1):** Adds a penalty equal to the absolute sum of the coefficients. This can result in zero coefficients, effectively eliminating some features from the model.

Implementing regularization in Python is straightforward with `sklearn`:

```
from sklearn.linear_model import LogisticRegression
```

```python

# Fit logistic regression model with L1 regularization
lasso_model = LogisticRegression(penalty='l1', solver='liblinear')
lasso_model.fit(X_train, y_train)

# Predict and evaluate
y_pred_lasso = lasso_model.predict(X_test)
print(classification_report(y_test, y_pred_lasso))
```

Conclusions of Logistic Regression

Logistic regression is one of the most widely used techniques for binary classification problems due to its simplicity and effectiveness. Understanding how it works, how to interpret its coefficients, and how to evaluate its performance are key skills for any professional working in the field of machine learning.

Decision Trees

Building Decision Trees

Decision trees are a popular technique in machine learning used for both classification and regression problems. This method employs a graphical and hierarchical approach to create a model that predicts the value of a response variable based on a series of decisions made from the features of the dataset. A decision tree resembles a flowchart where each internal node represents a test on a feature (attribute), each branch represents the outcome of that test, and each terminal node (leaf) represents a class (label) or a predicted value.

The construction of a decision tree is achieved through a recursive splitting process, where the feature providing the best separation of the data is repeatedly selected, and nodes with branches are generated that diverge towards different subsets of the original dataset. This process continues until a stopping criterion is met, such as node purity, the minimum number of samples required for a leaf, or the maximum tree depth.

How Does a Decision Tree Work?

To illustrate how a decision tree is built, let us consider the problem of forecasting whether a day will be sunny or rainy based on certain features such as temperature, humidity, and wind. The basic steps to construct a decision tree are:

1. **Feature Selection:** Evaluate all available features and choose the one that best separates the data into different classes. This is typically measured using metrics such as information gain, Gini impurity, or entropy impurity index.

2. **Dataset Splitting:** That feature is used to split the dataset into two or more subsets.

3. **Repetition:** For each resulting subset, the process is repeated from step 1 until one of the stopping criteria is met.

Example of Building a Decision Tree

Suppose we have a dataset containing information about the weather on various days and whether the day turned out to be sunny or rainy. The dataset might look as follows:

Temperature	Humidity	Wind	Sunny
High	High	No	No
High	High	Yes	No
Medium	High	No	Yes
Low	Medium	No	Yes
Low	Low	No	Yes
Low	Low	Yes	No
Medium	Low	Yes	Yes
High	Medium	No	No

Temperature	**Humidity**	**Wind**	**Sunny**
High	Medium	Yes	Yes
Medium	Medium	No	Yes

In this case, to build the decision tree, we evaluate each of the features (Temperature, Humidity, Wind) and calculate their capacity to separate sunny days from rainy days.

Let's assume that when calculating the Gini impurity, we find that the feature "Humidity" provides the best split. Thus, a node is created for "Humidity". Then, branching from this node, branches are created for the different classes of "Humidity" (High, Medium, Low), splitting the dataset accordingly, and the process is repeated for each resulting subset.

Here it might be helpful to illustrate how the tree would look as it is built. Finally, after repeating this splitting process, the tree could look something like this:

```
      Humidity
      /      |      \
   High   Medium    Low
    /        |        \
   No      Wind       Yes
           /   \
         No     Yes
```

Each leaf of the tree would represent a prediction of whether the day will be sunny or rainy.

Advantages and Disadvantages of Decision Trees

Advantages

1. **Easy to Interpret:** Decision trees are simple and easy to visualize. Their hierarchical structure allows users to easily understand how decisions are made.

2. **No Need for Data Scaling:** Unlike other algorithms, decision trees do not require feature scaling or normalization, meaning they can handle data of different scales without issues.

3. **Ability to Handle Categorical and Numerical Data:** Decision trees can manage both categorical and numerical data, making them flexible and applicable to a wide range of problems.

4. **Combination of Trees:** Multiple decision trees can be combined to create more robust models, such as in Random Forests, which helps improve accuracy and control overfitting.

Disadvantages

1. **Overfitting:** Decision trees are prone to overfitting, especially if the tree is very deep. This means they can fit too closely to the training data, resulting in poor performance on new data.

2. **Instability:** Small variations in the data can lead to a completely different tree being constructed. This can make decision trees unstable.

3. **Tendency to Follow Depth Connections:** Decision trees often

tend to follow patterns that may not be representative and consequently, may ignore interactions among features.

Pruning

A common technique to control overfitting in decision trees is pruning. Pruning involves removing branches from a decision tree that provide little information about the target class. By reducing the size of the tree, we can improve its generalization ability.

Types of Pruning

1. **Pre-Pruning:** Implemented during the tree-building process. At each step, it is evaluated whether adding a split actually improves the model according to a specific criterion. If it does not, the split is not made.
2. **Post-Pruning:** This is conducted after the full tree has been constructed. Each node is evaluated and a decision is made about whether it should be removed based on its impact on model accuracy.

Implementing a Decision Tree in Python

Below is an example of implementing a decision tree using the `scikit-learn` library. In this case, we will use the widely utilized Iris dataset in the machine learning community.

```
import pandas as pd
from sklearn.datasets import load_iris
```

```
from sklearn.model_selection import train_test_split
from sklearn.tree import DecisionTreeClassifier
from sklearn import tree
import matplotlib.pyplot as plt

# Load the Iris dataset
iris = load_iris()
X = iris.data
y = iris.target

# Split the dataset into training and testing sets
X_train, X_test, y_train, y_test = train_test_split(X, y,
 test_size=0.2, random_state=42)

# Create a decision tree
model = DecisionTreeClassifier(random_state=42)
model.fit(X_train, y_train)

# Evaluate the model
accuracy = model.score(X_test, y_test)
print(f'Model accuracy: {accuracy * 100:.2f}%')

# Visualize the decision tree
plt.figure(figsize=(12,8))
tree.plot_tree(model, filled=True, feature_names=iris.
feature_names, class_names=iris.target_names, rounded=True)
plt.title("Decision Tree for the Iris Dataset")
plt.show()
```

In this code, we load the Iris dataset, split it into a training set and a testing set, then fit a decision tree model. The model's accuracy is evaluated using the test set, and the tree is visualized using the `plot_tree` function.

Conclusion

Decision trees are a powerful and versatile technique in machine learning that allows for understanding and visualizing decision-making processes based on data. Due to their ability to handle both numerical and categorical data, they are applicable in many areas, from medicine to marketing. However, as with all machine learning models, it is crucial to be aware of their limitations, such as overfitting and instability, and to apply techniques like pruning to enhance their performance. As one progresses in machine learning, decision trees provide a solid foundation for understanding more complex and combinatorial techniques, such as Random Forests and Gradient Boosting.

Random Forest

Concept of Random Forest

Random Forest is a supervised learning algorithm used for both classification and regression tasks. Unlike individual decision trees, which can be highly susceptible to overfitting and data variability, Random Forest builds a "forest" of decision trees, each based on a random subset of training data and features. This approach helps improve the model's accuracy and robustness, turning a set of weak trees into a strong model.

The idea behind Random Forest can be summarized by the phrase "the wisdom of crowds," where a group of experts (in this case, decision trees) can make more accurate and reliable decisions than a single expert. By combining the predictions of multiple trees, Random Forest seeks to achieve a prediction that is less susceptible to the errors of individual trees.

How Does Random Forest Work?

Building a Random Forest model involves several key steps:

1. Creation of Decision Trees

The first step in creating a Random Forest is generating multiple decision trees. This is done using a method called **bootstrap aggregating** (or **bagging**), which involves the following steps:

- **Bootstrap Sampling:** A random subset of training data is drawn from the original dataset with replacement. This means that some instances may appear in the subset more than once, while others may not be present at all.

- **Tree Construction:** A decision tree is built using the sampled dataset. To decide on the splits in the tree, the algorithm randomly selects a subset of features instead of using all available features. This introduces diversity among the trees and helps mitigate overfitting.

This process is repeated to build multiple trees until a predefined number of trees is reached in the model.

2. Aggregation of Results

Once all the trees have been constructed, the next step is to make predictions. Depending on whether it is a classification or regression problem, the predictions are combined in different ways:

- **Classification:** In a classification task, each tree "votes" for a class, and the class with the most votes is selected as the final prediction of the model.

- **Regression:** In a regression task, the average of the predictions made by all the trees is taken to obtain the final prediction.

3. Handling Diversity

One key to the success of Random Forest is its ability to handle the diversity of the trees. By encouraging the use of different subsets of both data and features, the likelihood that all trees will make the same error is reduced. This variety among the trees strengthens the overall prediction of the model.

Advantages of Random Forest

Robustness Against Overfitting

One of the main advantages of Random Forest is its resistance to overfitting. Since the model consists of multiple trees that make independent decisions, the errors of a particular tree are largely compensated by the other trees in the forest. This results in more generalizable and robust models.

Handling Missing Data

Random Forest is capable of effectively handling missing data. If an instance in the dataset lacks information on a particular feature, the algorithm can use the values of other features to make a decision when necessary.

Feature Importance

Another important benefit of Random Forest is that it provides measures of feature importance. Through the process of building the trees, the algorithm can calculate how much each feature contributes to the predictions. This is useful for feature selection and for better understanding the model.

Disadvantages of Random Forest

Complexity

One disadvantage of Random Forest is that, while it is robust and accurate, it is also more complex and less interpretable than a single decision tree. Visualizing the complete model can be challenging due to the number of trees involved.

Training Time

Building a Random Forest can be slower than creating a single decision tree, especially if many trees are used in the model. This is because it requires generating and evaluating multiple trees.

Example of Random Forest in Python

Let's look at a practical example of how to implement a Random Forest model using the Iris dataset, which is one of the most commonly used datasets in the machine learning community.

First, we need to install the necessary libraries if you haven't already, such as pandas, scikit-learn, and matplotlib.

```
pip install pandas scikit-learn matplotlib
```

Now, let's implement a Random Forest model in Python:

```
import pandas as pd
import numpy as np
from sklearn.datasets import load_iris
from sklearn.model_selection import train_test_split
from sklearn.ensemble import RandomForestClassifier
from sklearn.metrics import classification_report,
 confusion_matrix
import matplotlib.pyplot as plt
import seaborn as sns

# Load the Iris dataset
iris = load_iris()
X = iris.data
y = iris.target

# Split the dataset into training and testing sets
X_train, X_test, y_train, y_test = train_test_split(X, y,
 test_size=0.2, random_state=42)

# Create a Random Forest model
modelo_rf = RandomForestClassifier(n_estimators=100,
 random_state=42)
modelo_rf.fit(X_train, y_train)

# Make predictions
y_pred = modelo_rf.predict(X_test)

# Evaluate the model
```

```
print("Confusion Matrix:")
print(confusion_matrix(y_test, y_pred))

print("\nClassification Report:")
print(classification_report(y_test, y_pred))

# Visualize Feature Importance
importancia = modelo_rf.feature_importances_
caracteristicas = iris.feature_names
indices = np.argsort(importancia)

plt.figure(figsize=(8, 6))
plt.title("Feature Importance")
plt.barh(range(len(caracteristicas)), importancia[indices], align='center')
plt.yticks(range(len(caracteristicas)), np.array(caracteristicas)[indices])
plt.xlabel("Importance")
plt.show()
```

Code Description

1. **Data Loading:** We use the Iris dataset, which contains information about three species of flowers.

2. **Splitting the Dataset:** We split the dataset into a training set and a testing set, using 20% as the test set.

3. **Model Creation:** We create a Random Forest model with 100 trees (`n_estimators=100`) and fit it to the training set.

4. **Predictions:** We make predictions on the test set.

5. **Model Evaluation:** We print the confusion matrix and the classification report, which help us evaluate the model's

performance.

6. **Feature Importance Visualization:** We graphically represent the importance of the features to understand which have the greatest impact on the predictions.

Conclusion

Random Forest is a powerful tool in the machine learning toolkit, thanks to its ability to build robust and accurate models by applying the wisdom of crowds. By combining multiple decision trees, it handles variability and overfitting better while providing valuable insights into feature importance.

With practice, Random Forest can become one of the most valuable tools in any data scientist's arsenal.

Support Vector Machines (SVM)

SVM Fundamentals

Support Vector Machines (SVM) are a powerful and versatile set of supervised learning techniques used for both classification and regression problems. The main idea behind SVM is to find a hyperplane that separates different classes of data in a high-dimensional space as effectively as possible.

To better understand this concept, let's imagine a scenario where we are trying to classify different types of fruits based on their characteristics, such as weight and size. Suppose we have two categories: apples and oranges. Each of these fruits has different characteristics that can be plotted in a graph where the X-axis represents weight and the Y-axis represents size. The task of SVM will be to find the best line (in this case, a hyperplane in two dimensions) that separates apples from oranges.

How SVM Works

When we talk about SVM, it is common to refer to two key concepts: the **separating hyperplane** and the **support vectors**.

Separating Hyperplane

A hyperplane is a line in two dimensions, a plane in three dimensions, and, in general, a structure of a space of dimension n-1 in an n-dimensional space. The idea is to find a hyperplane that maximizes the separation between different classes of data. In the context of SVM, the goal is to find the **optimal margin**, which is the widest distance between the hyperplane and the closest data points from both classes.

Support Vectors

The support vectors are the data points that are closest to the separating hyperplane. In fact, it is these points that determine the position and orientation of the hyperplane. If the support vectors are removed, the hyperplane could change, and therefore, the model's classification capability could degrade. This property is one of the reasons why SVM is so effective in classification challenges.

Separating Hyperplane and Optimal Margin

Mathematically, a hyperplane can be represented as:

$$w \cdot x + b = 0$$

Where:

- w is the weight vector, determining the orientation of the hyperplane.
- x is the input feature vector.
- b is the bias, determining the hyperplane's location in the space.

The goal of SVM is to maximize the distance between this hyperplane and the support vectors, which is defined as:

$$\text{Margin} = \frac{2}{\| w \|}$$

The problem can be posed as an optimization task, where we seek to minimize the loss function while satisfying the margin constraints.

Types of SVM

SVM can be classified into three main categories depending on the type of problem to be solved.

Linear SVM

When the data is linearly separable, linear SVMs are appropriate. In this case, there is a hyperplane that can completely separate the different classes. To find this hyperplane, the support vectors closest to it are used. The computational complexity of linear SVMs is relatively low, making them efficient for problems with a large number of samples.

Non-Linear SVM

However, in many cases, the data is not perfectly separable. This is where non-linear SVMs come into play. They use **kernels** to transform the data into a higher-dimensional space, where it becomes separable. The most common kernels are:

- **Linear Kernel:** Does not transform the data, used for linearly separable data.
- **Polynomial Kernel:** Transforms the data into a polynomial space of order n. Useful for non-linear classifications.
- **Gaussian (RBF) Kernel:** A radial kernel that allows for great flexibility by projecting the data into infinitely dimensional spaces.

The use of kernels allows non-linear SVMs to capture complex patterns in the data. However, this can also lead to increased computational complexity.

SVM for Regression

In addition to its use in classification, SVM can also be applied to regression tasks, known as **Support Vector Regression (SVR)**. Here, the goal is to fit a hyperplane instead of classifying the data. The idea is to find a margin that encapsulates as many data points as possible while minimizing errors. Just like in classification, support vectors play an important role in defining this margin.

Comparison of SVM with Other Algorithms

A distinctive feature of SVM is its ability to handle high-dimensional data effectively. Many classification algorithms, such as decision trees or logistic regression, can be adversely affected by too much dimensionality. However, SVM tends to perform well in those scenarios because it focuses only on the closest support vectors and not on the entirety of the data.

Additionally, SVM is less susceptible to overfitting issues compared to other methods. This is because it seeks to maximize the margin, which helps generalize the model.

Implementing SVM in Python

Below is an example of how to implement an SVM using the `scikit-learn` library in Python for a simple classification problem.

Classification Example with SVM

Suppose we are using the popular Iris dataset to classify different species of flowers. This dataset is a common benchmark to illustrate classification algorithms.

```
import numpy as np
import pandas as pd
from sklearn import datasets
from sklearn.model_selection import train_test_split
from sklearn.svm import SVC
from sklearn.metrics import classification_report, confusion_matrix
import matplotlib.pyplot as plt
from matplotlib import colors as mcolors

# Load the Iris dataset
iris = datasets.load_iris()
X = iris.data[:, :2]  # We will use only the first two features for visualization
y = iris.target

# Split the dataset into training and testing sets
X_train, X_test, y_train, y_test = train_test_split(X, y, test_size=0.3, random_state=42)

# Create the SVM model
```

```
model = SVC(kernel='linear')
model.fit(X_train, y_train)

# Predictions
y_pred = model.predict(X_test)

# Reporting Results
print(confusion_matrix(y_test, y_pred))
print(classification_report(y_test, y_pred))

# Visualizing the results
plt.figure(figsize=(10, 6))
colors = list(mcolors.TABLEAU_COLORS.values())
for i in range(len(np.unique(y))):
    plt.scatter(X[y == i, 0], X[y == i, 1], c=colors[i],
 label=iris.target_names[i])

# Define the range for the decision graph
xlim = plt.xlim()
ylim = plt.ylim()

# Create a mesh to visualize the decision boundary
xx = np.linspace(xlim[0], xlim[1], 100)
yy = np.linspace(ylim[0], ylim[1], 100)
YY, XX = np.meshgrid(yy, xx)
xy = np.vstack([XX.ravel(), YY.ravel()]).T
Z = model.decision_function(xy).reshape(XX.shape)

# Draw the decision boundary
plt.contourf(XX, YY, Z > 0, alpha=0.2, colors=colors)
plt.title('SVM with Linear Kernel')
plt.xlabel('Sepal Length')
plt.ylabel('Sepal Width')
plt.legend()
plt.show()
```

Code Description

1. **Loading the Dataset:** We utilize the Iris dataset from `scikit-learn`.

2. **Data Preparation:** We take the first two features of the dataset for a simple visualization. Then, we split the dataset into a training set and a testing set.

3. **Creating the SVM Model:** We initialize and train an SVM model using a linear kernel.

4. **Predictions and Evaluation:** We make predictions on the test set and display a classification report along with the confusion matrix.

5. **Visualizing Results:** We use `matplotlib` to visualize the data, decision boundaries, and the different types of flowers.

Conclusions

Support Vector Machines are a powerful and effective method for classification and regression problems. Their ability to handle high-dimensional data and their focus on maximizing the margin between classes make them highly effective. As they integrate into more applications, understanding how they work and how to implement SVM becomes an essential skill for the modern data scientist.

With the use of techniques like kernels, SVMs are flexible and can address complex problems that other algorithms may not be able to solve adequately. However, it is important to understand their limitations and apply them appropriately in contexts where they are most effective.

Introduction to Clustering

Clustering is a fundamental technique in the field of machine learning and data mining that is used to group a set of objects in such a way that the objects within the same group (or cluster) are more similar to each other than to those in other groups. Unlike classification, where categories are predefined, clustering is an unsupervised method that seeks to organize data into inherent patterns or structures without prior knowledge of labels.

Imagine we are biologists studying various species of plants. Without knowing the species in advance, we could take various measurements of the plants, such as leaf size, height, and number of flowers. Then, using clustering techniques, we could group the plants into clusters that reflect similarities, allowing us to uncover natural groupings in our data.

Importance of Clustering

Clustering has numerous applications in various fields, including:

- **Market Analysis:** Grouping customers into segments based on their purchasing behaviors and preferences.

- **Anomaly Detection:** Identifying unusual or atypical behaviors in data, such as fraudulent transactions in finance.
- **Image Segmentation:** Grouping pixels in an image for segmentation, facilitating the identification of objects.
- **Biology:** Grouping genes or proteins based on their expression patterns.

The versatility of clustering makes it a valuable tool for exploring, analyzing, and understanding data.

Types of Clustering

There are different approaches and clustering algorithms, each with its own characteristics and applications. Below, we will explore some of the most popular clustering methods.

Hierarchical Clustering

Hierarchical clustering creates a hierarchy of clusters that can be visually represented in a dendrogram. There are two main types of hierarchical clustering:

- **Agglomerative:** Starts with each object forming its own cluster and then iteratively combines the closest clusters until all objects are in a single cluster or a predefined number of clusters is reached.
- **Divisive:** Starts with all objects in a single cluster and iteratively divides it into smaller clusters.

This type of clustering is especially useful when trying to understand the hierarchical structure of data.

K-Means Clustering

K-Means is one of the most widely used clustering algorithms due to its simplicity and efficiency. The idea behind K-Means is to group a dataset into K clusters, where K is a parameter that must be defined by the user.

The K-Means process is carried out in several steps:

1. **Initialization:** Choose K random centroids from the data.
2. **Assignment:** Assign each data point to the cluster whose centroid is closest.
3. **Update:** Calculate new centroids as the average of all points in each cluster.
4. **Repetition:** Repeat steps 2 and 3 until the centroids stabilize or there are no changes in cluster assignments.

K-Means is straightforward and fast, but it is sensitive to the initial choice of centroids and the value of K. Methods such as **inertia** or the **elbow method** are often used to help determine the optimal number of clusters.

DBSCAN (Density-Based Spatial Clustering of Applications with Noise)

DBSCAN is a density-based clustering algorithm that allows for the identification of arbitrarily shaped clusters and is robust to noise and outliers. Unlike K-Means, which requires specifying the number of clusters, DBSCAN requires two parameters: the **maximum distance** `eps` that defines a point's neighborhood and the **minimum number of points** `min_samples` required to form a cluster.

The DBSCAN approach works as follows:

1. **Identify Core Points:** For each point, count the number of points within its neighborhood (`eps`).
2. **Form Clusters:** If a point has a sufficient number of neighbors, it is classified as a core point, and a cluster is formed around it.
3. **Expand Clusters:** Clusters are expanded to other points in the neighborhood that also meet the criteria.

DBSCAN is particularly good at detecting irregular cluster shapes and handling large volumes of data.

Clustering Evaluation

Evaluating the quality of clustering is crucial, as there are no predefined labels in an unsupervised dataset. Some common metrics for evaluating cluster quality include:

- **Silhouette Score:** Measures how well-separated the clusters are by calculating the difference between the average distance to points in the same cluster and the average distance to points in the nearest cluster. A high value indicates good separation.
- **Inertia:** Measures the sum of the squared distances of points to their corresponding centroid. Lower inertia values indicate more compact clusters.
- **Dendrograms:** In the case of hierarchical clustering, dendrograms allow for visualizing the relationship between clusters and their merging at different levels.

Implementing K-Means in Python

Let's implement K-Means in Python using the `scikit-learn` library with an example dataset. Consider that we are working with generated synthetic data.

```
import numpy as np
import matplotlib.pyplot as plt
from sklearn.datasets import make_blobs
from sklearn.cluster import KMeans
from sklearn.metrics import silhouette_score

# Generate synthetic data
X, y = make_blobs(n_samples=300, centers=4, cluster_std=
0.60, random_state=0)

# Visualize the generated data
plt.scatter(X[:, 0], X[:, 1], s=30)
plt.title('Synthetic Data')
plt.xlabel('Feature 1')
plt.ylabel('Feature 2')
plt.grid(True)
plt.show()

# Apply K-Means
kmeans = KMeans(n_clusters=4)
kmeans.fit(X)

# Retrieve cluster predictions
y_kmeans = kmeans.predict(X)

# Visualize the clustering results
plt.scatter(X[:, 0], X[:, 1], c=y_kmeans, s=30, cmap=
'viridis')
```

```
centers = kmeans.cluster_centers_
plt.scatter(centers[:, 0], centers[:, 1], c='red', s=200,
 alpha=0.75, marker='X')
plt.title('K-Means Clustering Results')
plt.xlabel('Feature 1')
plt.ylabel('Feature 2')
plt.grid(True)
plt.show()

# Calculate and display the Silhouette Score
silhouette_avg = silhouette_score(X, y_kmeans)
print(f'Silhouette Score: {silhouette_avg:.2f}')
```

Code Description

1. **Generation of Synthetic Data:** We use `make_blobs` to create a dataset with four clear groups.
2. **Data Visualization:** We plot the generated data to get an initial view before clustering.
3. **K-Means Application:** We initialize K-Means with four clusters and fit the model to our data.
4. **Prediction:** We obtain the cluster labels for each data point and visualize the results.
5. **Silhouette Score Calculation:** We measure how well-separated the clusters are by calculating the Silhouette Score.

Conclusion

Clustering is a powerful and versatile technique used in multiple disciplines to discover patterns and underlying structures in data. From market analysis to biology, its implementation can lead to significant discoveries. By understanding and applying different clustering algorithms, as well as evaluating their quality, value can be extracted from data in ways that drive informed decision-making and advancement in various areas of research and practice.

Advanced Clustering Techniques

Clustering is an essential technique in machine learning that allows for the grouping of unlabeled data into categories or clusters. After exploring the basic concepts of clustering, this chapter will focus on advanced techniques that offer more robust and flexible solutions for complex data clustering problems. As datasets become larger and more complex, it is crucial to have methods that can adapt to various situations and dimensions.

DBSCAN: Density-Based Clustering

DBSCAN (Density-Based Spatial Clustering of Applications with Noise) is a density-based clustering algorithm that allows for the identification of clusters of arbitrary shape, making it particularly useful in situations where clusters are not spherical or have irregular shapes. Unlike K-Means, which requires specifying the number of clusters beforehand, DBSCAN groups points based on the density of points in the space.

How Does DBSCAN Work?

DBSCAN uses two essential parameters to determine how it groups the data:

- **eps (epsilon):** The maximum distance between two points for them to be considered part of the same neighborhood.
- **min_samples:** The minimum number of points required to form a dense cluster.

The functioning process of DBSCAN can be summarized in the following steps:

1. **Core Points:** DBSCAN identifies points that have at least `min_samples` neighbors within the radius `eps`. These points are considered core points of a cluster.
2. **Cluster Expansion:** For each core point, the algorithm expands the cluster by joining all points that fall within the distance `eps`. This process repeats for new core points found during the expansion.
3. **Noise Points:** Points that do not meet the conditions to be part of any cluster are considered noise.

Example of DBSCAN in Python

Below is an example in Python that illustrates how to use the DBSCAN algorithm to cluster data:

```
import numpy as np
import matplotlib.pyplot as plt
from sklearn.datasets import make_moons
```

```
from sklearn.cluster import DBSCAN

# Generate synthetic moon-shaped data
X, _ = make_moons(n_samples=300, noise=0.05)

# Apply DBSCAN
dbscan = DBSCAN(eps=0.15, min_samples=5)
labels = dbscan.fit_predict(X)

# Visualize the results
plt.scatter(X[:, 0], X[:, 1], c=labels, cmap='viridis', s=
30)
plt.title('DBSCAN Clustering')
plt.xlabel('Feature 1')
plt.ylabel('Feature 2')
plt.grid(True)
plt.show()
```

In this code, we generate a dataset in the shape of a moon using `make_moons`, providing us with an ideal scenario where K-Means might fail due to the non-spherical shape of the data. We then apply the DBSCAN algorithm and plot the results, where different colors represent different clusters, and unclustered points are considered noise.

Advantages and Disadvantages of DBSCAN

Advantages:

- **Arbitrary Shape:** DBSCAN can identify clusters with arbitrary shapes, making it especially useful in applications where data is not distributed spherically.
- **Outlier Handling:** It performs well even in the presence of noise or outliers, identifying them as noise points that do not belong to any cluster.

Disadvantages:

- **Parameter Selection:** The choice of the `eps` and `min_samples` parameters can significantly influence the clustering result, and finding the right values may require testing and experimentation.
- **Density Sensitivity:** Variations in cluster density can lead to unexpected results, as DBSCAN's parameters are global and not adaptive.

Model-Based Clustering

Model-based clustering is another advanced technique used to group data. This approach models the underlying distribution of the data and uses a probability function to determine to which cluster each point belongs. One of the most common methods of model-based clustering is the **Gaussian Mixture Model (GMM)**.

Gaussian Mixture Models (GMM)

GMMs model the data as a combination of multiple Gaussian distributions. Each cluster is represented as a Gaussian distribution with its own parameters (mean and covariance matrix). The GMM model can capture the uncertainty in point assignment to clusters, unlike K-Means, which assigns points deterministically.

How GMM Works

The clustering process with GMM is carried out in the following steps:

1. **Initialization:** Set an initial assumption about the parameters of the Gaussian distributions (means, covariances, and proportions).

2. **Expectation-Maximization (EM):** Iterate between two steps:
    - **Expectation Step (E):** Calculate the probability that each point belongs to each of the clusters.
    - **Maximization Step (M):** Adjust the Gaussian distributions according to the calculated probabilities.
3. **Convergence:** Repeat the E and M steps until the parameters converge.

Example of GMM in Python

Here is an example of how to implement a Gaussian mixture model using the `scikit-learn` library:

```
import numpy as np
import matplotlib.pyplot as plt
from sklearn.datasets import make_blobs
from sklearn.mixture import GaussianMixture

# Generate synthetic data
X, _ = make_blobs(n_samples=300, centers=3, cluster_std=
0.60, random_state=0)

# Apply GMM
gmm = GaussianMixture(n_components=3)
gmm.fit(X)
labels = gmm.predict(X)

# Visualize the results
plt.scatter(X[:, 0], X[:, 1], c=labels, cmap='viridis', s=
30)
plt.title('GMM Clustering')
plt.xlabel('Feature 1')
```

```
plt.ylabel('Feature 2')
plt.grid(True)
plt.show()
```

In this example, we generate a synthetic dataset with three clusters and apply the GMM model. The resulting visualization shows how the algorithm identifies the clusters based on the Gaussian distributions fitted to the data.

Advantages and Disadvantages of GMM

Advantages:

- **Flexibility:** GMM can adapt the shape of clusters using Gaussian distributions, making it ideal for data with complex shapes.
- **Probability Assignment:** It can calculate the probability of a point belonging to a cluster, providing a richer interpretation compared to other algorithms.

Disadvantages:

- **Parameter Tuning:** Selecting the number of components and initialization can be problematic, and like K-Means, GMM requires that the number of clusters be defined in advance.
- **Sensitivity to Initial Values:** Like other clustering methods, GMM can be sensitive to the initial values of its parameters, which can lead to suboptimal results.

Spectral Clustering

Spectral clustering is another advanced approach that utilizes spectral properties of matrices associated with the data to perform clustering. It is often used to detect non-convex clusters and allows for discovering complex structures in the data.

How Spectral Clustering Works

1. **Constructing the Adjacency Matrix:** Build a matrix that represents the similarities or distances between data points.
2. **Calculating the Laplacian Matrix:** From the adjacency matrix, the Laplacian matrix can be calculated, which captures the connectivity structure of the data.
3. **Calculating Eigenvalues and Eigenvectors:** Perform spectral decomposition of the Laplacian matrix, allowing for the identification of the principal components that best describe the data distribution.
4. **Clustering in Reduced Space:** Apply a clustering method, typically K-Means, in the reduced space represented by the selected eigenvectors.

Example of Spectral Clustering in Python

The following example illustrates how to perform spectral clustering using `scikit-learn` on a synthetic dataset:

```
import numpy as np
import matplotlib.pyplot as plt
from sklearn.datasets import make_moons
from sklearn.cluster import SpectralClustering

# Generate synthetic data
X, _ = make_moons(n_samples=300, noise=0.05)

# Apply spectral clustering
```

```
spectral = SpectralClustering(n_clusters=2, affinity='nearest_neighbors')
labels = spectral.fit_predict(X)

# Visualize the results
plt.scatter(X[:, 0], X[:, 1], c=labels, cmap='viridis', s=30)
plt.title('Spectral Clustering')
plt.xlabel('Feature 1')
plt.ylabel('Feature 2')
plt.grid(True)
plt.show()
```

In this example, we generate a synthetic dataset in the shape of a moon and apply spectral clustering to identify the two shapes, which present non-convex separation.

Advantages and Disadvantages of Spectral Clustering

Advantages:

- **Non-Convex Model:** It can handle clusters of any shape and is particularly effective for complex data relationships.
- **Robust to Irregularities:** Its ability to leverage connectivity information makes it competent even in the presence of noise.

Disadvantages:

- **Computational Complexity:** Calculating eigenvalues and eigenvectors can be computationally intensive and more time-consuming than other methods.
- **Parameter Sensitivity:** Like many algorithms, its results can

depend on the choice of hyperparameters, such as the similarity strategy.

Conclusions

As datasets become more complex, it is necessary to approach clustering with advanced techniques that can capture the underlying structure of the data. Techniques such as DBSCAN, GMM, and spectral clustering provide powerful tools for grouping data of varied shapes and handling noise and complexity.

By understanding and applying these advanced methods, data scientists can extract valuable insights from unlabeled data, opening new opportunities for exploration and data analysis across multiple domains.

Bayesian Models

Introduction to Bayesian Theory

Bayesian models are a category of statistical models that apply Bayes' theorem to update the probability of a hypothesis as new data becomes available. This perspective is rooted in the intuitive principle that prior information can be combined with new evidence to form a more informed conclusion. As data accumulates, Bayesian models allow for more robust inferences and predictions.

Bayes' theorem can be expressed mathematically as:

$$P(H \mid D) = \frac{P(D \mid H) \cdot P(H)}{P(D)}$$

Where:

- $P(H \mid D)$ is the posterior probability of the hypothesis H given the data D.

- $P(D \mid H)$ is the probability of observing the data D given that H is true (likelihood).
- $P(H)$ is the prior probability of the hypothesis H.
- $P(D)$ is the probability of observing the data D under all possible hypotheses.

Intuitive Example of Bayes' Theorem

Imagine we are trying to diagnose a disease in a population. Suppose that:

- The disease has a prevalence of 1% in the population (this is $P(H) = 0.01$).
- If a person has the disease, there is a 90% probability that they will test positive (this is $P(D \mid H) = 0.9$).
- The test can yield a positive result in 5% of healthy individuals (this is $P(D \mid \neg H) = 0.05$).

We want to know the probability that someone actually has the disease given that their test result is positive ($P(H \mid D)$).

Using Bayes' theorem, we can calculate $P(D)$ using the law of total probability:

$$P(D) = P(D \mid H) \cdot P(H) + P(D \mid \neg H) \cdot P(\neg H)$$

Now we insert the values:

$$P(D) = (0.9 \cdot 0.01) + (0.05 \cdot 0.99) = 0.009 + 0.0495 = 0.0585$$

Then, we apply Bayes' theorem:

$$P(H \mid D) = \frac{P(D \mid H) \cdot P(H)}{P(D)} = \frac{0.9 \cdot 0.01}{0.0585} \approx 0.154$$

Therefore, there is approximately a 15.4% probability that a person has the disease given a positive test result. This example illustrates how Bayes' theorem allows us to update our beliefs based on new evidence.

Bayesian Models in Practice

Bayesian models provide a flexible framework that can be applied to a wide variety of problems, from classification to prediction in uncertain situations. These models are particularly valuable in contexts where prior information is limited or where it is desired to explicitly incorporate uncertainty into the analysis.

Bayesian Parameter Estimation

In many cases, Bayesian models are used to estimate unknown parameters in a model from observed data. This process involves selecting a likelihood function for the data and a prior distribution for the parameters.

For example, consider a simple linear regression model:

$y = \beta_0 + \beta_1 x +$ �

where � follows a normal distribution. In this model, β_0 and β_1 are the parameters we wish to estimate. The Bayesian estimation would involve assuming prior values for these parameters and then updating those beliefs based on the observed data.

Bayesian Inference

Bayesian inference refers to the process of making inferences about the distributions of parameters of interest after observing the data. The key in Bayesian inference is that, from the prior information and the likelihood of the data, we obtain the posterior distribution of the parameters.

To calculate the posterior distribution of the parameters θ, we use Bayes' theorem:

$$P(\theta \mid D) = \frac{P(D \mid \theta) \cdot P(\theta)}{P(D)}$$

MCMC Methods (Markov Chain Monte Carlo)

Often, the posterior distribution is difficult to calculate directly. This is where sampling methods like MCMC come into play, allowing us to approximate the posterior distribution by sampling points in the parameter space.

MCMC is based on generating a chain of samples where each point depends on the previous one. This allows exploring the characteristics of the posterior distribution without needing to calculate it explicitly.

Bayesian Models in Machine Learning

In the context of machine learning, Bayesian models have gained popularity for their ability to handle sparse data, incorporate uncertainty, and adapt models as new information becomes available. Here are some examples of how they are used:

Bayesian Classifiers

Bayesian classifiers, such as Naive Bayes, are used for text classification, spam detection, and other classification problems. The main idea behind the Naive Bayes classifier is to assume that features are independent of each other given the class value.

The probability that a document belongs to a class can be calculated as:

$$P(C \mid D) \propto P(C) \prod_i P(w_i \mid C)$$

where $P(C)$ is the prior probability of the class and $P(w_i \mid C)$ is the probability that a feature w_i appears given that the class is C.

Bayesian Networks

Bayesian networks are an extension of Bayesian models that represent a set of variables and their conditional dependencies through a directed acyclic graph (DAG). These networks are made up of nodes (variables) and edges (dependencies) that describe the probabilistic relationship between the variables.

Bayesian networks are useful for modeling complex problems involving multiple variables and dependency relationships. They allow making inferences about one or more variables based on available observations and provide a framework for analyzing how evidence affects inferences.

Evaluation of Bayesian Models

Evaluating Bayesian models can be challenging due to the probabilistic nature of the inference involved. However, there are several metrics and techniques that can be used to assess their performance:

Prediction and Comparison

Comparing Bayesian models may involve evaluating accuracy, coverage, and generalization capability. It is common to split data into training and testing sets or use cross-validation methods to assess the predictive performance of a model.

Bayesian Information

Bayesian information criteria, such as the **Bayesian Information Criterion (BIC)** or the **Akaike Information Criterion (AIC)**, are often used to compare and select Bayesian models. These metrics penalize for model complexity and help balance fit and simplicity.

Cross-Validation

Cross-validation, commonly used in machine learning, is also applied in the Bayesian context. It allows assessing how a model generalizes to new data and helps avoid overfitting by partitioning the data into training and testing sets.

Implementing a Bayesian Model in Python

Let's see a simple example using `scikit-learn`, where we will create a Naive Bayes classifier for a dataset on flowers, specifically the Iris dataset.

```
import numpy as np
import pandas as pd
from sklearn.datasets import load_iris
from sklearn.model_selection import train_test_split
from sklearn.naive_bayes import GaussianNB
from sklearn.metrics import classification_report,
 confusion_matrix

# Load the Iris dataset
iris = load_iris()
X = iris.data
y = iris.target
```

```
# Split the dataset into training and testing sets
X_train, X_test, y_train, y_test = train_test_split(X, y, test_size=0.2, random_state=42)

# Create the Naive Bayes classifier
gnb = GaussianNB()
gnb.fit(X_train, y_train)

# Make predictions
y_pred = gnb.predict(X_test)

# Evaluate the model
print("Confusion Matrix:")
print(confusion_matrix(y_test, y_pred))

print("\nClassification Report:")
print(classification_report(y_test, y_pred))
```

Code Description

1. **Data Loading:** We load the Iris dataset available in `scikit-learn`.
2. **Data Split:** We split the data into a training set and a testing set.
3. **Classifier Creation:** We initialize and fit a Naive Bayes classifier.
4. **Predictions:** We make predictions on the testing set.
5. **Evaluation:** We print the confusion matrix and classification report to assess the model's performance.

Conclusion

Bayesian models provide a powerful and flexible framework for analysis and inference in uncertain situations. Their ability to incorporate prior information and update beliefs based on new data makes them particularly valuable in machine learning. Through examples such as the Naive Bayes classifier and Bayesian networks, we can see the practical application of these concepts in various areas, from classification to complex decision-making.

As technology advances and new data is generated, Bayesian models will continue to be essential tools for extracting information and making inferences in an increasingly complex world.

Model Evaluation

Model evaluation is a critical stage in the development of machine learning systems. While creating an effective model is essential, it is equally important to ensure that the model is functioning properly and is capable of generalizing to unseen new data. In this chapter, we will explore the main metrics and techniques used to evaluate machine learning models, with a focus on classification and regression.

Fundamentals of Model Evaluation

Model evaluation is based on the principle of comparing the model's outputs with the actual or expected values. To carry out this comparison, test datasets are used, which are samples of data that were not used during the model's training. This ensures that the evaluation metrics reflect the model's ability to generalize and not just its effectiveness in memorizing the training data.

Training, Validation, and Test Sets

Before diving into evaluation metrics, it's fundamental to understand how data is divided into training, validation, and test sets:

- **Training Set:** This is the subset of data used to fit the model. During training, the model learns patterns from these samples.
- **Validation Set:** This is a part of the data used to tune hyperparameters and make decisions about the model (such as when to stop training in techniques like early stopping). It should not be used during training.
- **Test Set:** This is the final subset used to evaluate the model's performance once it has been trained and tuned. It must be completely independent of the training and validation sets.

Properly separating the datasets is essential to avoid overfitting, where a model fits too closely to the training data and loses its ability to generalize.

Evaluation Metrics for Classification

In classification problems, there are several common metrics used to quantify a model's performance. The most relevant metrics include:

Accuracy

Accuracy is the proportion of correct predictions to the total number of predictions made. It is a simple and widely used metric, but can be misleading if the data is imbalanced (i.e., if there are many more instances of one class than another).

$$\text{Accuracy} = \frac{\text{TP+TN}}{\text{TP+TN+FP+FN}}$$

Where:

- TP: True Positives
- TN: True Negatives
- FP: False Positives
- FN: False Negatives

Precision, Recall, and F1-Score

In addition to accuracy, it is crucial to consider other metrics such as **precision** and **recall**. Precision measures the proportion of true positives over the total predicted positives:

$$\text{Precision} = \frac{\text{TP}}{\text{TP+FP}}$$

Recall measures the proportion of true positives over the total actual positives:

$$\text{Recall} = \frac{\text{TP}}{\text{TP+FN}}$$

The **F1-Score** is the harmonic mean of precision and recall, providing a single metric that considers both aspects:

$$F1 = 2 \cdot \frac{\text{Precision} \cdot \text{Recall}}{\text{Precision+Recall}}$$

The F1-Score is particularly useful when there is an imbalance in the classification data.

Confusion Matrix

The confusion matrix is a powerful tool that provides a more detailed view of the model's performance by showing the count of true positives, true negatives, false positives, and false negatives. It allows for better evaluation of the model's predictions, differentiation between classes, and understanding where it may be failing.

The confusion matrix has the following form:

	Positive Prediction	Negative Prediction
Actual Positive	TP	FN
Actual Negative	FP	TN

ROC Curves and AUC

The **ROC Curve** (Receiver Operating Characteristic) is a graphical representation that illustrates a model's performance across different classification thresholds. In this curve, the X-axis represents the false positive rate (FP), while the Y-axis represents the true positive rate (TP).

The **Area Under the ROC Curve (AUC)** provides a single metric that evaluates performance across all thresholds. An AUC of 1 indicates a perfect model, while an AUC of 0.5 indicates a model that is no better than random chance.

Evaluation Example in Python

Let's look at a practical example of how to evaluate a classification model using the concepts discussed above. We will use the Iris dataset to create a classification model.

```
import numpy as np
import pandas as pd
import seaborn as sns
import matplotlib.pyplot as plt
```

```
from sklearn.datasets import load_iris
from sklearn.model_selection import train_test_split
from sklearn.naive_bayes import GaussianNB
from sklearn.metrics import classification_report,
 confusion_matrix, roc_curve, auc

# Load the Iris dataset
iris = load_iris()
X = iris.data
y = iris.target

# Split the dataset into training and testing sets
X_train, X_test, y_train, y_test = train_test_split(X, y,
 test_size=0.2, random_state=42)

# Create the Naive Bayes classifier
gnb = GaussianNB()
gnb.fit(X_train, y_train)

# Make predictions
y_pred = gnb.predict(X_test)

# Evaluate the model
print("Confusion Matrix:")
print(confusion_matrix(y_test, y_pred))

print("\nClassification Report:")
print(classification_report(y_test, y_pred))


# ROC Curves (only works in binary problems, so we convert
to binary)

y_test_binary = (y_test == 0).astype(int)
# Considering only class 0
```

```python
y_pred_proba = gnb.predict_proba(X_test)[:, 0]  # Probabilities for class 0

fpr, tpr, thresholds = roc_curve(y_test_binary, y_pred_proba)
roc_auc = auc(fpr, tpr)

# Plot the ROC curve
plt.figure(figsize=(10, 6))
plt.plot(fpr, tpr, color='blue', label=f'AUC = {roc_auc:.2f}')
plt.plot([0, 1], [0, 1], color='red', linestyle='--')
plt.title('ROC Curve')
plt.xlabel('False Positive Rate')
plt.ylabel('True Positive Rate')
plt.grid(True)
plt.legend()
plt.show()
```

Evaluation Metrics for Regression

In regression problems, evaluation metrics differ and focus on measuring the difference between predicted values and actual values. Here are some of the most common metrics:

Mean Absolute Error (MAE)

The mean absolute error is the average of the absolute differences between predicted values and actual values. It is an intuitive and easy-to-interpret metric.

$$MAE = \frac{1}{n} \sum_{i=1}^{n} \mid y_i - \hat{y}_i \mid$$

Mean Squared Error (MSE)

The mean squared error is similar to MAE, but it penalizes larger errors more, as the differences are squared.

$$MSE = \frac{1}{n}\sum_{i=1}^{n}(y_i - \hat{y}_i)^2$$

Root Mean Squared Error (RMSE)

The root mean squared error is simply the square root of the MSE and returns the measure to the original scale of the data:

$$RMSE = \sqrt{MSE}$$

R^2 (Coefficient of Determination)

R^2 measures the proportion of total variation in the data that is explained by the model. An R^2 of 1 indicates that the model explains all variability, whereas an R^2 of 0 indicates that it explains nothing.

$$R^2 = 1 - \frac{SS_{res}}{SS_{tot}}$$

Where:

- $SS_{res} = \sum_{i=1}^{n}(y_i - \hat{y}_i)^2$ is the sum of squared errors.
- $SS_{tot} = \sum_{i=1}^{n}(y_i - \bar{y})^2$ is the total sum of squared errors relative to the mean.

Evaluation Example in Python for Regression

Now let's see a practical example for evaluating a linear regression model using the Boston Housing dataset.

```
import numpy as np
import pandas as pd
import matplotlib.pyplot as plt
from sklearn.datasets import load_boston
from sklearn.model_selection import train_test_split
from sklearn.linear_model import LinearRegression
from sklearn.metrics import mean_absolute_error,
 mean_squared_error, r2_score

# Load the Boston Housing dataset
boston = load_boston()
X = boston.data
y = boston.target

# Split the dataset into training and testing sets
X_train, X_test, y_train, y_test = train_test_split(X, y,
 test_size=0.2, random_state=42)

# Create the linear regression model
model = LinearRegression()
model.fit(X_train, y_train)

# Make predictions
y_pred = model.predict(X_test)

# Evaluate the model
mae = mean_absolute_error(y_test, y_pred)
mse = mean_squared_error(y_test, y_pred)
rmse = np.sqrt(mse)
r2 = r2_score(y_test, y_pred)

print(f'Mean Absolute Error (MAE): {mae:.2f}')
print(f'Mean Squared Error (MSE): {mse:.2f}')
```

```
print(f'Root Mean Squared Error (RMSE): {rmse:.2f}')
print(f'Coefficient of Determination (R²): {r2:.2f}')

# Plot Predictions vs Actual Values
plt.scatter(y_test, y_pred)
plt.plot([y.min(), y.max()], [y.min(), y.max()], color=
'red', linestyle='--')
plt.xlabel('Actual Values')
plt.ylabel('Predictions')
plt.title('Predictions vs Actual Values')
plt.grid(True)
plt.show()
```

Conclusions

Model evaluation is a vital component of the model development process in machine learning. Through appropriate metrics and solid evaluation practices, valuable insights into model performance and generalization capabilities can be obtained. As you advance in your journey in the field of artificial intelligence, mastering these metrics and understanding their importance in this ever-evolving context is essential. Ultimately, a well-evaluated model is not only more effective but also more reliable and useful in real-world applications.

Feature Engineering

Feature engineering is a fundamental process in the development of machine learning models. It involves transforming and selecting the variables that will feed the learning algorithms in order to improve their performance and generalization ability. A good feature set can make the difference between a mediocre model and an exceptional one. In this chapter, we will explore what feature engineering is, why it is important, and how various techniques can be applied to enhance the data to be used.

Importance of Feature Engineering

In machine learning, models are only as good as the data they receive. Once a dataset has been collected, the next step is to prepare it for learning. This can include cleaning the data, selecting the most relevant features, transforming them, or creating new features from existing ones. Good feature engineering not only increases the accuracy of the model, but also reduces the risk of overfitting, improves the interpretability of the model, and accelerates training time.

Imagine we are developing a model to predict housing prices. If we have features such as the number of rooms, location, and area, these may be useful. However, if we transform the location into a categorical variable, or if we create a new feature that represents the relationship between the size of the house and the number of rooms, it is very likely that the model will learn more complex patterns and generalize better.

Creating New Features

Creating new features, also known as **feature engineering**, involves combining or transforming existing features to generate additional useful information for the model. Here are some common techniques for creating additional features:

Mathematical Transformations

Sometimes, applying mathematical functions to features can help highlight patterns in the data. For example:

- **Logarithms**: Applying a logarithmic transformation to variables that have a skewed distribution can help normalize them.
- **Powers**: Creating square or cubic variables can help capture non-linear relationships.

Example in Python

Suppose we have a dataset about cars with features such as price and engine power. We can apply a logarithmic transformation to the price to normalize it:

```
import pandas as pd
import numpy as np

# Create a sample DataFrame
data = {'price': [5000, 15000, 30000, 50000], 'power': [80,
  100, 120, 150]}
df = pd.DataFrame(data)

# Apply logarithmic transformation
df['log_price'] = df['price'].apply(lambda x: np.log(x))
print(df)
```

Feature Combination

New features can also be created by combining two or more variables. For example, if you have the area of a lot and the number of floors of a house, you can create a new feature that represents the total built area.

```
# Create a sample DataFrame with area and number of floors
data = {'lot_area': [200, 300, 150, 400], 'num_floors': [1, 2
  , 1, 3]}
df = pd.DataFrame(data)

# Create combined feature
df['total_area'] = df['lot_area'] * df['num_floors']
print(df)
```

Feature Interaction

Feature interaction refers to creating new variables that represent the interaction between two or more variables. This can be important in models that do not naturally capture these relationships.

```
# Create a DataFrame with sample variables
data = {'age': [25, 30, 35, 40], 'income': [30000, 40000,
  50000, 60000]}
df = pd.DataFrame(data)

# Create a new feature that represents the interaction
df['age_income'] = df['age'] * df['income']
print(df)
```

Feature Engineering Technologies: Tools and Libraries

There are various Python tools and libraries that facilitate feature engineering. Below, we will explore some of the most useful:

Pandas

Pandas is the reference library in Python for data manipulation and analysis. It provides powerful data structures and functions that make the creation and transformation of features straightforward and efficient.

Scikit-learn

Scikit-learn is not only useful for model training but also has preprocessing tools that are essential for feature engineering. Some of these tools include:

- **PolynomialFeatures**: Generates polynomial features from existing features.

- **OneHotEncoder**: Converts categorical variables into dummy variables that can be used in models.

```
from sklearn.preprocessing import PolynomialFeatures,
    OneHotEncoder

# Example of using PolynomialFeatures
poly = PolynomialFeatures(degree=2)
X_poly = poly.fit_transform(df[['age', 'income']])
print(X_poly)

# Example of using OneHotEncoder
encoder = OneHotEncoder()
X_encoded = encoder.fit_transform(df[['category']])
    # Assuming 'category' is a categorical variable
```

Featuretools

Featuretools is a Python library specifically designed for the automated creation of features. It allows users to build new features from existing ones through an "automated feature engineering" approach.

Variable Selection

Variable selection involves identifying and retaining only the features that are truly relevant to the model. Dimensionality reduction can help improve model performance and interpretability. Some techniques for variable selection include:

Filter-Based Methods

Filter methods evaluate the relevance of features using statistical metrics without using a specific model. Examples of filter metrics include correlation, p-values, and other measures of association.

Wrapper-Based Methods

Wrapper methods utilize a model to evaluate combinations of features. These methods are often more accurate but also more computationally expensive. Examples include forward and backward search methods.

Embedded Methods

Embedded methods combine the benefits of filter and wrapper approaches. They use a learning model to perform feature selection during the training process. A common example is using Lasso (L1 regression), which penalizes model complexity and can lead to the removal of some features.

```
from sklearn.linear_model import Lasso
from sklearn.pipeline import make_pipeline
from sklearn.preprocessing import StandardScaler

# Assuming X_train, y_train are our training data
lasso = Lasso(alpha=0.1)
model = make_pipeline(StandardScaler(), lasso)
model.fit(X_train, y_train)

# Get coefficients
coef = lasso.coef_
print(coef)
```

Variable Transformation

Variable transformation is an additional step that can help improve the quality of features. This includes techniques such as:

Normalization and Standardization

Normalization (scaling variables to range from 0 to 1) and standardization (scaling variables to have mean 0 and standard deviation 1) are common methods to make features comparable in magnitude.

```
from sklearn.preprocessing import MinMaxScaler,
    StandardScaler

# Normalization
scaler = MinMaxScaler()
X_normalized = scaler.fit_transform(X)

# Standardization
scaler = StandardScaler()
X_standardized = scaler.fit_transform(X)
```

Transformation of Categorical Variables

Categorical variables must be transformed into a format that can be understood by models. This includes the creation of dummy variables, which was previously mentioned in the feature engineering technologies section.

```
# Transform categorical variable to dummy variables
```

```
df_dummies = pd.get_dummies(df['category'], drop_first=True)
df = pd.concat([df, df_dummies], axis=1)
```

Conclusions

Feature engineering is a crucial part of developing machine learning models. Through the creation and transformation of features, as well as the selection of the most relevant ones, data scientists can significantly enhance the performance of their models. The tools and techniques described in this chapter provide a solid foundation for performing feature engineering effectively and ethically. As you advance in your artificial intelligence projects, remember that careful attention to feature engineering can be the key to the success of your models.

Variable Selection

Variable selection is a fundamental process in the field of machine learning that involves identifying and retaining the most relevant features for the model. As datasets grow in size and complexity, having a systematic approach to select the variables that actually provide useful information for the model's predictions becomes crucial. A well-selected set of features can lead to better model performance, greater interpretability, and a reduction in the risk of overfitting.

Importance of Variable Selection

Variable selection is critical for several reasons:

- **Improvement of Model Performance:** By reducing the number of features to the most relevant ones, the complexity of the model decreases, which can lead to better prediction results. A simpler model tends to generalize better on unseen data.
- **Reduction of Training Time:** Fewer features mean fewer

calculations, allowing for faster and more efficient training. This is especially important when working with large datasets.

- **Interpretability:** A model with fewer features is easier to interpret. This allows analysts and decision-makers to better understand how the variables influence the outcomes.

- **Prevention of Overfitting:** An excess of features can lead the model to fit too closely to the training data, resulting in poor performance on new data. Variable selection helps mitigate this risk.

Methods of Variable Selection

There are several approaches to variable selection, which can generally be classified into three categories: filter-based methods, wrapper-based methods, and embedded methods.

Filter-Based Methods

Filter methods evaluate the relevance of each variable individually, and the selection is based on this assessment. This approach does not use a specific model for selection. Some examples of metrics that can be used include correlation, p-values, mutual information, and chi-squared tests.

- **Correlation:** The correlation between each feature and the target variable can be calculated. Features that show a strong correlation with the target variable are selected.

- **Chi-Squared Test:** This method is commonly used for categorical variables. It assesses whether there is a significant relationship between two categorical variables.

Example of Filter-Based Method in Python

Below is an example of how correlation can be used to select relevant variables.

```
import pandas as pd
import numpy as np

# Create a sample DataFrame
data = {
    'feature1': np.random.rand(100),
    'feature2': np.random.rand(100),
    'feature3': np.random.rand(100) * 2 + 1, # More correlated with target variable
    'target': np.random.randint(0, 2, 100) # Binary target variable
}
df = pd.DataFrame(data)

# Calculate correlations
correlations = df.corr()
print(correlations['target'].sort_values(ascending=False))
```

Wrapper-Based Methods

Wrapper methods use a machine learning model to evaluate the performance of a specific subset of features. These methods are generally more accurate but require more computational time, as they involve fitting the model multiple times.

- **Forward Selection:** It starts with an empty set and adds features in the order of their performance until a certain threshold is reached.

- **Backward Selection:** It begins with all features and sequentially removes the least relevant ones.

Example of Wrapper-Based Method in Python

Below, we show an example of forward selection using `scikit-learn`.

```
from sklearn.datasets import load_iris
from sklearn.model_selection import train_test_split
from sklearn.linear_model import LogisticRegression
import itertools

# Load the Iris dataset
iris = load_iris()
X = iris.data
y = iris.target

def forward_selection(X, y):
    n_features = X.shape[1]
    best_features = []
    best_score = 0

    for i in range(1, n_features + 1):
        for feature_combo in itertools.combinations(range(n_features), i):
            X_subset = X[:, feature_combo]
            X_train, X_test, y_train, y_test = train_test_split(X_subset, y, test_size=0.2, random_state=42)
            model = LogisticRegression()
            model.fit(X_train, y_train)
            score = model.score(X_test, y_test)

            if score > best_score:
```

```
                best_score = score
                best_features = feature_combo

    return best_features

best_features = forward_selection(X, y)
print(f'Best features: {best_features}')
```

Embedded Methods

Embedded methods are a combination of filter and wrapper approaches. They utilize a machine learning model as part of their operation during the training process. A common technique in this group is Lasso regularization, which penalizes the complexity of the model and can lead some coefficients to become zero.

Example of Embedded Method in Python

Here is an example of feature selection using Lasso.

```
from sklearn.linear_model import Lasso
from sklearn.datasets import load_boston
from sklearn.preprocessing import StandardScaler
from sklearn.pipeline import make_pipeline

# Load the Boston Housing dataset
boston = load_boston()
X = boston.data
y = boston.target

# Normalize the features
```

```
pipeline = make_pipeline(StandardScaler(), Lasso(alpha=0.1))
pipeline.fit(X, y)

# Get coefficients
lasso_coef = pipeline.named_steps['lasso'].coef_
print("Lasso Coefficients:", lasso_coef)
```

Evaluation of Variable Selection

After applying feature selection, it is crucial to evaluate its effectiveness. This can be done by comparing the performance of the model using the original set of variables versus the selected set of variables. Common metrics to evaluate this performance include accuracy, F1-score for classification, and MAE, MSE for regression.

Example of Evaluation

```
from sklearn.model_selection import train_test_split
from sklearn.linear_model import LogisticRegression
from sklearn.metrics import classification_report

# Suppose we have a dataset
X_train, X_test, y_train, y_test = train_test_split(X, y,
 test_size=0.2, random_state=42)

# Using all features
model_full = LogisticRegression()
model_full.fit(X_train, y_train)
y_pred_full = model_full.predict(X_test)

print("Classification Report with all variables:")
```

```python
print(classification_report(y_test, y_pred_full))

# Using only selected features
X_train_selected = X_train[:, best_features]
X_test_selected = X_test[:, best_features]

model_selected = LogisticRegression()
model_selected.fit(X_train_selected, y_train)
y_pred_selected = model_selected.predict(X_test_selected)

print("Classification Report with selected features:")
print(classification_report(y_test, y_pred_selected))
```

Conclusions

Variable selection is a fundamental stage in the development of machine learning models. By choosing the most relevant features, one can improve model performance, speed up training time, and enhance interpretability. Variable selection methods, which include filters, wrappers, and embedded approaches, provide various options to tackle this challenge. Ultimately, careful variable selection will lead to more accurate and effective models that can deliver valuable solutions across numerous fields.

Variable Transformation

Variable transformation is a crucial step in the data preprocessing process in machine learning. It involves modifying the features of a dataset to improve the quality of the information that will be fed into the model. Transformations can help address issues such as non-normal distribution, feature scaling, and handling categorical variables. In this chapter, we will explore some of the most common techniques for transformation and their importance in the modeling process.

Importance of Variable Transformation

Transforming variables is essential for several reasons:

- **Improves Normality:** Many machine learning algorithms, especially those based on regression, assume that the data follows a normal distribution. Variable transformation can help meet this assumption.
- **Feature Scaling:** Different features may have different scales,

which can affect the performance of some models. Scaling features ensures they have the same influence on the model.

- **Handling Categorical Variables:** Categorical variables are common in datasets and must be transformed into a format that can be understood by machine learning algorithms.
- **Reduction of Multicollinearity:** Some transformations, such as creating polynomial features, allow capturing interactions and nonlinear relationships between variables, which can be useful in building more complex models.

Normalization and Standardization

Two of the most common techniques for transforming variables are normalization and standardization. Both are used to scale features and make them comparable.

Normalization

Normalization refers to transforming features so that their values fall within a specific range, typically from 0 to 1. This is achieved using the following formula:

$$X' = \frac{X - X_{min}}{X_{max} - X_{min}}$$

Normalization is especially useful when working with distance-based algorithms, such as K-Means and K-Nearest Neighbors.

```
import pandas as pd
from sklearn.preprocessing import MinMaxScaler

# Create an example DataFrame
```

```python
data = {'feature1': [100, 200, 300, 400, 500],
        'feature2': [10, 15, 20, 25, 30]}
df = pd.DataFrame(data)

# Apply normalization
scaler = MinMaxScaler()
normalized_data = scaler.fit_transform(df)

print("Normalized Data:")
print(normalized_data)
```

Standardization

Standardization, also known as Z-score normalization, transforms features to have a mean of 0 and a standard deviation of 1. The formula used is:

$$X' = \frac{X-\mu}{\sigma}$$

where μ is the mean and σ is the standard deviation. Standardization is particularly useful for algorithms that assume data follows a normal distribution.

```python
from sklearn.preprocessing import StandardScaler

# Create an example DataFrame
data = {'feature1': [10, 20, 30, 40, 50],
        'feature2': [5, 15, 25, 35, 45]}
df = pd.DataFrame(data)

# Apply standardization
scaler = StandardScaler()
standardized_data = scaler.fit_transform(df)

```

```
print("Standardized Data:")
print(standardized_data)
```

Transformation of Categorical Variables

In many datasets, categorical variables play an important role. However, these types of variables are not directly usable in many machine learning algorithms. Therefore, it is necessary to convert them into a format that models can understand.

Dummy Variables

One of the most common ways to transform categorical variables is by using dummy variables. This technique creates new columns in the dataset, where each category is converted into a binary column (0 or 1) indicating the presence or absence of that category in an observation.

```
# Create an example DataFrame with a categorical variable
data = {'color': ['red', 'green', 'blue', 'red', 'green']}
df = pd.DataFrame(data)

# Create dummy variables
df_dummies = pd.get_dummies(df['color'], drop_first=True)
  # drop_first prevents the dummy variable trap
df = pd.concat([df, df_dummies], axis=1)

print("DataFrame with Dummy Variables:")
print(df)
```

Ordinal Encoding

Sometimes, categorical variables have a natural order (e.g., low, medium, high). In these cases, ordinal encoding can be used to represent these categories with numeric values according to their order.

```
# Create an example DataFrame with an ordinal categorical variable
data = {'size': ['small', 'medium', 'large', 'medium']}
df = pd.DataFrame(data)

# Encoding mapping
size_mapping = {'small': 1, 'medium': 2, 'large': 3}
df['encoded_size'] = df['size'].map(size_mapping)

print("DataFrame with Ordinal Encoding:")
print(df)
```

Advanced Transformation Techniques

Logarithmic Transformations

Logarithmic transformations are useful for dealing with variables that have a skewed distribution or that vary by orders of magnitude. Applying a logarithmic transformation can help normalize the data and facilitate modeling.

```
import numpy as np
```

```
# Create an example DataFrame
data = {'currency': [1, 10, 100, 1000, 10000]}
df = pd.DataFrame(data)

# Apply logarithmic transformation
df['log_currency'] = df['currency'].apply(lambda x: np.log(x)
  )

print("DataFrame with Logarithmic Transformation:")
print(df)
```

Power Transformation

Power transformation, such as squaring or cubing, can capture nonlinear relationships that may not be evident with the original features. This technique is effective in contexts where the relationship between variables is presumed to be nonlinear.

```
# Create an example DataFrame
data = {'feature': [1, 2, 3, 4, 5]}
df = pd.DataFrame(data)

# Apply power transformation
df['feature_squared'] = df['feature'] ** 2

print("DataFrame with Power Transformation:")
print(df)
```

Conclusions

Variable transformation is an essential component of data preprocessing in machine learning. By applying normalization techniques, standardization, and specific transformations, the quality and utility of features in a dataset can be significantly improved. These steps not only facilitate learning effective patterns for the models but also contribute to the interpretability and overall performance of the model. As always, it is essential to consider the context and nature of the data when choosing the most appropriate transformations for each situation. As you advance in your artificial intelligence projects, remember that good variable transformation can make a difference in your results.

Introduction to Optimization Techniques

Optimization is a fundamental pillar in the practice of machine learning. Its goal is to find the optimal parameters of a model that minimize or maximize a target function. In this chapter, we will explore the fundamentals of optimization, the main associated algorithms, and their relevance in machine learning. We will learn how these techniques are used to adjust models, improve their performance, and ensure that they generalize adequately on new data.

Fundamentals of Optimization

Optimization, in simple terms, refers to the process of adjusting something to make it the best it can be within certain constraints or conditions. When applying this to machine learning, we are seeking the parameters of a model that minimize the loss function. This loss function measures how far the predictions of our model are from the actual values.

Imagine we are trying to adjust a road through a series of mountains. The road represents our model parameters, and the mountains are the errors (or losses) we are trying to minimize. Optimization is the process of finding the smoothest and most efficient route through those hills, that is, finding a way to minimize the total travel cost on that road.

Objective Function

The objective function is what we want to optimize. In the context of machine learning, this is usually the loss function. For example, in a regression problem, a common loss function is the Mean Squared Error (MSE), which is calculated as:

$$L(\theta) = \frac{1}{n} \sum_{i=1}^{n} (y_i - \hat{y}_i)^2$$

where y_i are the actual values, $\hat{y}_i$ are the model predictions, and θ represents the model parameters. The idea is to find the values of θ that minimize $L(\theta)$.

Common Optimization Algorithms

There are several optimization algorithms that are commonly used in training machine learning models. Below are some of the most popular ones:

Gradient Descent

Gradient descent is the most widely used optimization algorithm in the field of machine learning. The basic idea behind this method is to update the model parameters in the opposite direction of the gradient of the loss function.

The gradient of the loss function is given by the vector of partial derivatives that indicate the direction of steepest ascent. To minimize the loss function, we need to move in the opposite direction of this vector.

Parameter Update

Parameters are updated using the following rule:

$$\theta = \theta - \alpha \nabla L(\theta)$$

where α is the learning rate, and $\nabla L(\theta)$ is the gradient of the loss function with respect to the parameters.

Example of Gradient Descent in Python

We can implement simple gradient descent in a linear regression problem to see how it works in practice.

```
import numpy as np
import matplotlib.pyplot as plt

# Generate some example data
np.random.seed(0)
X = 2 * np.random.rand(100, 1)
y = 4 + 3 * X + np.random.randn(100, 1)

# Initialize parameters
theta = np.random.randn(2, 1)  # two parameters: intercept and slope
learning_rate = 0.01
n_iterations = 1000
m = len(y)
```

```python

# Cost function to compute MSE
def compute_cost(X_b, y, theta):
    return (1 / (2 * m)) * np.sum((X_b.dot(theta) - y) ** 2
)

# Add a column of 1s for the intercept term
X_b = np.c_[np.ones((m, 1)), X]
# Adds 1s in the first column

# Apply gradient descent
for iteration in range(n_iterations):
    gradients = (1 / m) * X_b.T.dot(X_b.dot(theta) - y)
    theta = theta - learning_rate * gradients
    if iteration % 100 == 0:
        cost = compute_cost(X_b, y, theta)
        print(f"Iteration {iteration}, cost: {cost}")

# Visualize the fitted line
plt.scatter(X, y)
plt.plot(X, X_b.dot(theta), color='red', linewidth=2)
plt.xlabel("X")
plt.ylabel("y")
plt.title("Linear Regression Fit")
plt.show()
```

Variants of Gradient Descent

There are several variants of gradient descent that are used to improve efficiency and convergence:

Stochastic Gradient Descent (SGD)

In SGD, instead of calculating the gradient using the entire dataset, individual samples (or minibatches) are used to update the parameters. This introduces noise into the optimization process, which can help escape local minima and boost convergence towards a global minimum.

Mini-Batch Gradient Descent

This approach combines the batch and stochastic gradient descent methods. Small batches of data are used to compute the gradient, providing a balance between the variability of SGD and the stability of batch gradient descent.

Enhanced Gradient Descent Variants

- **Momentum:** This approach uses past gradients to smooth out the current updates. Thus, if the direction of the updates stays the same, the model picks up greater speed in that direction.
- **Adam (Adaptive Moment Estimation):** This algorithm combines the advantages of SGD and RMSProp, adaptively managing the learning rate for each parameter and using first and second-order moments of the gradient.

Second-Order Optimization Algorithms

Second-order optimization algorithms calculate the second derivative (Hessian) instead of just the gradient. These methods are more efficient in terms of convergence but are computationally more expensive.

- **Newton's Method:** Uses the Hessian to find the minimum more directly, but requires computing and storing the Hessian matrix, which may be impractical for large datasets.
- **L-BFGS:** A more efficient algorithm that approximates the Hessian and is more suitable for large problems.

Importance of Optimization in Machine Learning

Optimization plays a crucial role in model fitting in machine learning. The quality of the solutions that algorithms find largely depends on the optimization algorithm used and the correct configuration of the learning rate and other hyperparameters.

Common Challenges in Optimization

During optimization, a number of challenges may be encountered, such as:

- **Overfitting:** A model may fit too closely to the training data, losing its ability to generalize. This can be mitigated through techniques such as regularization.
- **Local Minima:** In non-convex loss functions, optimization algorithms may converge to suboptimal solutions. Techniques like SGD can be used to address this.
- **Learning Rate:** A learning rate that is too high may cause the algorithm to diverge, while a rate that is too low may result in very long convergence times.

Strategies to Improve Optimization

To improve the results of optimization, the following strategies can be considered:

- **Experiment with Learning Rate:** Finding an optimal learning rate is critical. This may involve conducting a search or using automated tuning algorithms.
- **Implement Regularization:** Regularization techniques such as L1 and L2 can help avoid overfitting, stabilizing the optimization process.
- **Use Acceleration and Adaptation Techniques:** Implementing methods such as Momentum or Adam can significantly increase convergence efficiency.

Conclusions

Optimization is an essential part of the model training process in machine learning. Understanding the main optimization algorithms, objective functions, and tuning strategies is crucial for ensuring robust and effective models. By applying improvements and recognizing common optimization challenges, practitioners can maximize the performance of their models and their ability to generalize on unseen data. With the right knowledge about optimization techniques, you are prepared to tackle complex challenges in the field of artificial intelligence, allowing for significant advancements in the development of intelligent and effective solutions.

Data Preprocessing Strategies

Data preprocessing is an essential step in the machine learning model development process. Before data is fed into a model, it is crucial to ensure that it is in a clean and useful format. Preprocessing may include data cleaning, handling missing values, encoding categorical variables, and other necessary transformations. In this chapter, we will explore the main data preprocessing strategies that every data scientist should know to build effective and efficient models.

Importance of Data Preprocessing

The quality of data significantly impacts the performance of machine learning models. If the data is not well-prepared, even the most advanced algorithm can produce unsatisfactory results. This is because many machine learning algorithms perform better with data that is clean, normalized, and properly structured.

The most common analogy used is that of cooking: just as a chef carefully selects and prepares ingredients before starting to cook, data scientists must prepare their data before training a model. Without proper preprocessing, the "ingredients" of the dataset can lead to "dishes" (models) that do not taste good.

Data Cleaning

Data cleaning involves identifying and correcting errors or inconsistencies in the dataset. This may include removing or imputing missing values, correcting typographical errors, and removing duplicates.

Identifying Missing Values

Missing values are common in real-world datasets and can occur for various reasons, such as failures in data collection or errors in data entry. The presence of missing values can cause issues when training a model, as many algorithms cannot handle missing data.

Example in Python

Below is how to identify missing values in a Pandas DataFrame.

```
import pandas as pd

# Create a sample DataFrame with missing values
data = {
    'age': [25, 30, None, 35, 40],
    'income': [50000, None, 60000, 70000, 80000],
    'nationality': ['USA', 'USA', 'CAN', None, 'MEX']
```

```
}
df = pd.DataFrame(data)

# Identify missing values
print("Missing Values in each column:")
print(df.isnull().sum())
```

Handling Missing Values

Once identified, decisions must be made about what to do with missing values. Several strategies exist:

- **Row Deletion:** In some cases, removing rows with missing values may be a viable option, especially if it is a small proportion of the dataset.

```
# Remove rows with any missing values
df_cleaned = df.dropna()
print("DataFrame after removing rows with missing values:")
print(df_cleaned)
```

- **Value Imputation:** An alternative is to impute (fill) the missing values with methods such as the mean, median, or mode of the column. This can be useful to avoid losing too much data.

```
# Impute the mean for age and income
df['age'].fillna(df['age'].mean(), inplace=True)
df['income'].fillna(df['income'].mean(), inplace=True)

print("DataFrame after imputation:")
print(df)
```

Handling Duplicates

Duplicates can introduce noise into the model and negatively affect its performance. Therefore, it is essential to identify and remove them if found.

```
# Create a sample DataFrame with duplicates
data = {
    'name': ['John', 'Ana', 'John', 'Luis', 'Ana'],
    'age': [25, 30, 25, 35, 30]
}
df_duplicates = pd.DataFrame(data)

# Remove duplicates
df_duplicates = df_duplicates.drop_duplicates()
print("DataFrame after removing duplicates:")
print(df_duplicates)
```

Handling Missing Data

Missing data can arise for various reasons, and how it is handled can have a significant impact on the performance of the model.

Imputation

Imputation involves filling in the missing data with some statistical strategy. In addition to the mean or median, there are other more complex techniques, such as K-Nearest Neighbors imputation or using regression models to predict the missing values.

Example of Imputation Using Scikit-Learn

```
from sklearn.impute import SimpleImputer

# Create an imputer to fill missing values with the mean
imputer = SimpleImputer(strategy='mean')

# The imputer needs to be fitted to the data before use
df[['age', 'income']] = imputer.fit_transform(df[['age',
  'income']])
```

Encoding Categorical Variables

Machine learning algorithms often require categorical variables to be converted into a numerical format. Several techniques exist for this:

One-Hot Encoding

One-hot encoding is a common technique that converts a categorical variable into a set of binary variables, one for each category. This avoids ordering issues and allows models to interpret categorical variables correctly.

```
# One-Hot Encoding
df_one_hot = pd.get_dummies(df, columns=['nationality'],
  drop_first=True)
print("DataFrame after One-Hot Encoding:")
print(df_one_hot)
```

Ordinal Encoding

Sometimes, categorical variables may have an inherent order (e.g., 'low', 'medium', 'high'). In these cases, ordinal encoding may be appropriate, assigning numerical values based on the order of the categories.

```
# Encoding mapping
ord_mapping = {'low': 1, 'medium': 2, 'high': 3}
df['quality'] = ['low', 'medium', 'high', 'medium', 'low']
    # Example of quality
df['quality_encoded'] = df['quality'].map(ord_mapping)

print("DataFrame after ordinal encoding:")
print(df[['quality', 'quality_encoded']])
```

Feature Scaling Strategies

Feature scaling is another important step in preprocessing, as different features may have different scales that affect model performance.

Normalization

Normalization, which we have explored previously, scales the features of a dataset to a range between 0 and 1. This is particularly useful for algorithms that use distance metrics, such as K-Nearest Neighbors.

Standardization

Standardization transforms the features to have a mean of 0 and a standard deviation of 1. This is beneficial for many algorithms, especially those that assume normality in the data.

```
from sklearn.preprocessing import StandardScaler

# Create a sample DataFrame
data = {'income': [50000, 60000, 70000, 80000, 90000]}
df_scaling = pd.DataFrame(data)

# Standardize
scaler = StandardScaler()
df_scaling['standardized_income'] = scaler.fit_transform(
  df_scaling[['income']])
print("DataFrame after standardization:")
print(df_scaling)
```

Conclusions

Data preprocessing is a critical step in developing machine learning models. Through techniques of cleaning, handling missing data, encoding categorical variables, and scaling features, data scientists can prepare high-quality datasets that increase the likelihood of generating accurate and effective models. Careful attention to this process can not only improve model performance but also ensure that it is based on ethical and representative data. As you progress in the field of machine learning, remembering the importance of solid preprocessing will be key to your success.

Data Visualization

Data visualization is an essential component of data analysis and machine learning model development. Through graphs and images, data scientists can communicate findings, discover hidden patterns and trends, observe data distribution, and facilitate result interpretation. Visualization not only serves to present information but also acts as a powerful tool for data exploration. In this chapter, we will explore the importance of data visualization, the most commonly used tools, and how to apply effective techniques to create representative graphs.

Importance of Data Visualization

Data visualization should not be seen as merely a collection of graphs; it is a critical process that brings multiple benefits:

- **Effective Communication:** The ability to represent complex data simply and understandably allows different audiences, from experts to general public, to interpret findings easily.

- **Identification of Patterns and Trends:** Visualization helps identify patterns, correlations, and trends that may not be obvious in raw data tables. This is particularly useful during the exploratory data analysis (EDA) phase.
- **Anomaly Detection:** By visualizing data, analysts can detect outliers or anomalies that could negatively impact machine learning models.
- **Support in Decision-Making:** Data visualization provides a solid foundation for decision-making by offering a clear overview of what the data is communicating.

Imagine a salesperson studying their customer data. An appropriate graph could reveal that sales increase during certain months of the year, allowing them to plan marketing strategies accordingly.

Visualization Tools: Matplotlib and Seaborn

There are many libraries in Python for data visualization, but Matplotlib and Seaborn are two of the most popular and powerful.

Matplotlib

Matplotlib is a highly versatile 2D visualization library that allows for the creation of high-quality, customizable graphs. Its flexibility makes it ideal for creating a wide range of visualizations, from simple line graphs to scatter and bar plots.

Example Usage of Matplotlib

To illustrate how to use Matplotlib, let's consider an example where we visualize the sales of different products over a year.

```
import matplotlib.pyplot as plt

# Sample data
products = ['Product A', 'Product B', 'Product C',
  'Product D']
sales = [1500, 2500, 3000, 2000]

# Create a bar chart
plt.bar(products, sales, color=['blue', 'orange', 'green',
  'red'])
plt.title('Product Sales in a Year')
plt.xlabel('Products')
plt.ylabel('Sales')
plt.show()
```

This simple code creates a bar chart representing the sales of different products, using colors to distinguish between categories.

Seaborn

Seaborn is a library built on top of Matplotlib that makes it easier to create attractive and complex visualizations. Seaborn provides a more user-friendly and aesthetically pleasing interface, as well as statistical graphs that are easier to implement.

Example Usage of Seaborn

Suppose we want to visualize the relationship between the length and width of the sepals in the famous Iris dataset. Seaborn allows us to create a scatter plot with different colors for each flower species:

```python
import seaborn as sns
import pandas as pd
from sklearn.datasets import load_iris

# Load the Iris dataset
iris = load_iris()
df = pd.DataFrame(data=iris.data, columns=iris.feature_names)
df['species'] = iris.target

# Visualize the relationship between sepal lengths and widths
sns.scatterplot(data=df, x='sepal length (cm)', y=
  'sepal width (cm)', hue='species', palette='Set1')
plt.title('Sepal Scatter Plot - Iris Dataset')
plt.show()
```

This scatter plot allows us to observe how Iris species group based on their characteristics, providing useful information about the differences among them.

Creating Representative Graphs

When it comes to data visualization, there are certain considerations regarding how to create representative graphs:

Selection of the Graph Type

Choosing the right type of graph depends on the nature of the data and the message that needs to be communicated. Some examples include:

- **Line Graphs:** Useful for showing trends over time, such as month-to-month sales performance.
- **Bar Graphs:** Ideal for comparing quantities across different

categories.

- **Scatter Plots:** Effective for observing the relationship between two variables and detecting patterns.
- **Box Plots:** Suitable for visualizing distributions and detecting outliers.

Customization of Graphs

One of the advantages of Matplotlib and Seaborn is the ability to customize graphs. This includes adjusting colors, line styles, labels, and titles, as well as adding legends and annotations. For example:

```
plt.bar(products, sales, color=['skyblue', 'lightcoral',
   'lightgreen', 'orange'])
plt.title('Product Sales in a Year', fontsize=14)
plt.xlabel('Products', fontsize=12)
plt.ylabel('Sales', fontsize=12)
plt.grid(axis='y', linestyle='--', alpha=0.7)
plt.show()
```

Customization makes graphs more appealing and the information easier to interpret.

Annotations and Legends

Including annotations on graphs is essential to highlight key points. For example, stripes, labels, or text boxes can be added to explain specific data points. Legends are equally important, as they help readers understand what each category represents in a graph.

```
plt.bar(products, sales)
plt.title('Product Sales in a Year')
for i, v in enumerate(sales):
    plt.text(i, v + 50, str(v), ha='center')
plt.show()
```

In this example, we have added labels that show the exact sales for each product.

Advanced Visualization Techniques

In addition to basic graphs, there are advanced techniques that allow for more complex and meaningful visualizations:

- **Heatmaps:** Useful for observing correlations and distributions in data.
- **Interactive Visualizations:** Using libraries like Plotly or Bokeh to create interactive graphs that allow the user to explore the data.
- **Surface Plots:** Ideal for representing three-dimensional relationships between variables.

Example of a Heatmap

```
import numpy as np
import seaborn as sns

# Create a correlation matrix
data = np.random.rand(10, 12)
correlation_matrix = np.corrcoef(data, rowvar=False)
```

```python

# Generate a heatmap
sns.heatmap(correlation_matrix, annot=True, cmap='coolwarm')
plt.title('Correlation Heatmap')
plt.show()
```

Conclusions

Data visualization is an indispensable tool in data analysis and machine learning. It not only enhances communication and interpretation of results but also allows for the discovery of patterns and trends that can influence decision-making. As you continue to work in artificial intelligence and machine learning, remembering the importance of visualizing your data will help you build more effective models and present your findings convincingly. With the right tools and a focus on clarity and precision, data visualization can transform the way you interact with information.

Ethical Considerations in Machine Learning

Machine learning has transformed numerous aspects of modern life, from recommendation systems on streaming platforms to algorithms that assist in medical diagnoses. Despite its undeniable benefits, the implementation of these technologies involves facing significant ethical challenges. In this chapter, we will explore the ethical considerations related to machine learning, focusing on data bias, transparency and accountability in decision-making, and the regulations and best practices that should be followed.

Importance of Ethics in Machine Learning

Ethics in machine learning is fundamental because automated decisions can have a profound impact on people's lives. A biased algorithm can result in harmful decisions that perpetuate social, economic, or other injustices. Thus, it is crucial that data professionals and model developers consider the implications of their creations and work to ensure that artificial intelligence

(AI) benefits society as a whole, rather than a specific group at the expense of others.

Let us imagine a case where a candidate selection system for a job uses a machine learning algorithm. If the data used to train the model reflect gender or racial bias, the system may inadvertently favor certain groups, contributing to discrimination.

Data Bias

One of the main ethical issues in machine learning is bias in the data. Algorithms often learn patterns from the data they were trained on, and if that data contains biases, the model will reflect and potentially amplify those biases.

Origins of Bias

Biases can arise from various sources:

- **Selection Bias:** When the data is not representative of the general population. For example, a dataset from an insurance company that mostly includes men may result in a model that discriminates against women or specific age groups.

- **Measurement Bias:** When the characteristics used to train the model are poorly defined or poorly measured, leading to incorrect interpretations. For instance, measuring academic performance in a way that favors a specific demographic group.

- **Confirmation Bias:** When the data reflects pre-existing beliefs or expectations that were confirmed during data collection. This can occur if the data is collected with the intention of testing a hypothesis rather than exploring a phenomenon without prejudice.

Consequences of Bias

Biases can lead to unfair and unethical decisions in critical contexts, such as access to credit, healthcare treatments, and job opportunities. For example, a credit system that penalizes certain racial minorities could limit their access to loans, thereby perpetuating social and economic inequalities.

Example: COMPAS

A notorious case of bias in machine learning is the COMPAS system used in the U.S. judicial system. This system was designed to predict the likelihood of a criminal reoffending. However, research has shown that the model tends to be more lenient with white offenders than with black offenders, despite equivalent criminal behaviors. This has sparked intense debate regarding the ethics of using risk algorithms in the judicial system.

Transparency and Accountability

Transparency in how machine learning models function is essential for building trust and ensuring accountability. A lack of transparency can lead to misunderstandings about how decisions are made and increased skepticism from those impacted by these automated decisions.

Importance of Transparency

Complex operational models, such as deep neural networks, are often considered "black boxes" because it is difficult to understand how they make decisions. This raises the issue of "ethical accountability," which is the ability to attribute decisions to systems.

Example: Model Explainability

To address transparency, various techniques can be used to explain the decisions of models. For example, decision tree models are more interpretable and allow tracing how a final decision derives from input characteristics.

However, even in complex models, tools such as LIME (Local Interpretable Model-agnostic Explanations) or SHAP (SHapley Additive exPlanations) can be utilized to provide explanations of predictions in terms understandable to humans. This enhances understanding and trust in the models.

Accountability Requirements

It is essential for organizations that develop and use machine learning models to establish clear accountability mechanisms. These may include:

- **Regular Audits:** Conducting community audits and reviews of the algorithm to assess its performance and biases.
- **Detailed Documentation:** Keeping records of how models were trained, the data used, and the strategic decisions made during model development.

Regulations and Best Practices

Given the growing concern about the ethical implications of machine learning, it is essential to have regulations and best practices to guide its development and application.

Emerging Regulations

Regulations related to AI and machine learning are on the rise as governments and international organizations seek to establish frameworks to ensure ethical practices. An example of this is the General Data Protection Regulation (GDPR) in the European Union, which requires companies to be transparent about how they use personal data and provides individuals rights regarding their data.

Recommended Best Practices

For developers and data scientists, some recommended practices include:

- **Involve Diverse Stakeholders:** Ensuring that diverse voices are represented in model development can help mitigate biases in its formulation and evaluation.
- **Conduct Testing with Diverse Data:** Testing the model with data from different demographic groups can provide valuable insights into how the model performs with different populations.
- **Foster Open Communication:** Creating an environment where teams involved in model development can share ethical concerns and openly discuss potential solutions.

Conclusions

Ethical considerations in machine learning are fundamental to ensuring that technology is used for the benefit of society. Identifying and mitigating biases in data, promoting transparency, and establishing clear standards are crucial steps that data scientists and organizations must follow to create fair and responsible AI systems. As we move toward an increasingly algorithm-driven world, ethics must be at the center of our decisions on how to develop, implement, and regulate these systems. The responsibility lies not only with those who create algorithms but also with those who use them and with society as a whole, to ensure that artificial intelligence benefits everyone equitably.

Common Challenges in Machine Learning

Machine learning, despite its great potential and popularity, faces a series of challenges that can complicate the development and implementation of effective models. As we explore these challenges, we will focus on issues of overfitting and underfitting, scalability difficulties, and some practical strategies to overcome them. Understanding these obstacles is crucial for any professional who seeks to navigate the landscape of machine learning and create effective and sustainable artificial intelligence solutions.

Overfitting and Underfitting

One of the most common challenges in machine learning is the balance between a model's overfitting and underfitting. Both phenomena negatively affect the model's generalization to new data.

Overfitting

Overfitting occurs when a model becomes too tailored to the training dataset. This means that the model captures not only the general trends but also the noise and random fluctuations of the dataset. As a result, the model performs well initially on training data, but its performance on unseen data degrades significantly.

Example of Overfitting

Imagine you are training a model to predict house quality based on features such as size, number of rooms, and location. If you decide to use a high-degree polynomial model, the model may fit perfectly to all the data points in the training set, but when you try to make predictions about new houses, the model may fail and provide incorrect results.

Visually, this can be represented with a curve that overly fits all points on a graph, generating a fitting line that rises and falls dramatically:

```
import numpy as np
import matplotlib.pyplot as plt
from sklearn.preprocessing import PolynomialFeatures
from sklearn.linear_model import LinearRegression

# Generate sample data
np.random.seed(0)
X = 5 * np.random.rand(50, 1)
y = 2 + 3 * X + np.random.randn(50, 1)

# Train a 15-degree polynomial model
poly = PolynomialFeatures(degree=15)
X_poly = poly.fit_transform(X)
```

```
model = LinearRegression()
model.fit(X_poly, y)

# Plot the data and the model's curve
plt.scatter(X, y, color='blue', label='Data')
X_fit = np.linspace(0, 5, 100).reshape(-1, 1)
y_fit = model.predict(poly.transform(X_fit))
plt.plot(X_fit, y_fit, color='red', label=
'Polynomial Model (Overfitting)')
plt.title('Example of Overfitting')
plt.xlabel('X')
plt.ylabel('y')
plt.legend()
plt.show()
```

Underfitting

Underfitting, on the other hand, occurs when a model is too simple to capture the underlying trends in the data. This means that the model performs poorly on both the training data and unseen data. An underfitted model lacks the necessary capacity to learn the complexity of the data.

Example of Underfitting

Returning to the same house quality example, if you decided to use simple linear regression (a straight line) to model the relationship between the house features and its quality, you are likely to fail to capture the variability of the data. This translates to a model that does not fit well either to the training data or to new data:

```
# Train a linear regression model
```

```
from sklearn.linear_model import LinearRegression

model_linear = LinearRegression()
model_linear.fit(X, y)

# Plot the data and the model's line
plt.scatter(X, y, color='blue', label='Data')
y_fit_linear = model_linear.predict(X)
plt.plot(X, y_fit_linear, color='green', label=
    'Linear Model (Underfitting)')
plt.title('Example of Underfitting')
plt.xlabel('X')
plt.ylabel('y')
plt.legend()
plt.show()
```

Strategies to Mitigate Overfitting and Underfitting

Here are some strategies you can employ to tackle overfitting and underfitting:

- **Regularization:** Techniques such as L1 (Lasso) and L2 (Ridge) are used to penalize model complexity, thus maintaining a balance between fitting and simplicity.
- **Early Stopping:** In deep learning, you can monitor the model's performance on a validation set and stop training when the performance begins to degrade.
- **Cross-Validation:** Use cross-validation methods to assess the model's generalization ability across different partitions of the dataset. This can help you identify when a model is capable of generalizing well.
- **Hyperparameter Tuning:** Perform a hyperparameter search to

optimize modeling configurations, such as the number of layers in a neural network or the degree of a polynomial.

Scalability Challenges

As datasets increase in size and complexity, scalability becomes a significant challenge in machine learning. Some algorithms may not efficiently handle large volumes of data, limiting their practical applicability.

Example of Scalability

Consider a competing recommendation system that analyzes billions of transactions daily. An algorithm that works well for a small dataset could become impractical or ineffective when applied to a significantly larger volume. Operations may become slow or require memory consumption that exceeds available resources.

Strategies to Improve Scalability

- **Use of Mini-Batches/Minibatch Training:** Instead of processing the entire dataset, working with mini-batches can make training more manageable and efficient.
- **Sampling-Based Algorithms:** Use techniques such as SMOTE (Synthetic Minority Over-sampling Technique) to create synthetic examples that can help balance uneven classes without the need to process large volumes of data.
- **Use of Distributed Techniques:** Implement tools like Apache Spark or Dask, which allow distributing the workload across multiple nodes, thereby improving the efficiency of data processing.

- **Resource Optimization:** Leverage specialized hardware like GPUs for training deep learning models, which can significantly accelerate calculations.

Conclusions

Navigating the challenges in machine learning is essential for developing effective and robust models. By understanding overfitting and underfitting, as well as scalability difficulties, data scientists can make informed decisions that optimize model performance. Implementing appropriate strategies will ensure that models are not only accurate but also equipped to handle the complexity and volume of data encountered in real-world scenarios. As you advance in your career in artificial intelligence, remember that overcoming these challenges can make the difference between a model that meets expectations and one that truly impacts its field of application.

Data Exploration and Analysis

Data exploration and analysis are fundamental steps in the machine learning lifecycle. Before training a model, it's crucial to understand the data that will be used. This includes understanding its nature, distribution, patterns, and any anomalies it may contain. In this chapter, we will explore exploratory data analysis (EDA) methods, appropriate visualization techniques, and how tools like Pandas and NumPy can facilitate this process.

Importance of Data Exploration

Imagine you are tasked with designing a marketing strategy for a new product line. Before deciding which market segments to target, you would want to know your target audience: What are their preferences? What products have been successful in the past? By applying a similar approach in data analysis, you can gain valuable insights that will guide all your subsequent decisions. Data exploration allows you to:

- **Uncover Hidden Patterns:** Often, data contains patterns and relationships that are not immediately apparent. EDA can reveal correlations between different variables, which can help build more effective models.

- **Identify Anomalies and Outliers:** The presence of outliers can indicate errors in the data or interesting phenomena that deserve attention. Early identification of these can prevent a model from learning from misleading data.

- **Guide Data Preparation:** By better understanding the data, informed decisions can be made regarding necessary preprocessing, such as imputing missing values, transforming variables, and feature engineering.

Exploratory Data Analysis Methods

There are various techniques that can be applied during the EDA stage. Here, we will present some of the most common ones:

Descriptive Statistical Summary

A critical first step in EDA is obtaining a summary of the descriptive statistics of our data. This includes the mean, median, mode, standard deviation, and percentiles of each variable, providing an initial overview of the dataset.

In Python, using Pandas, a basic statistical summary can be easily obtained:

```
import pandas as pd

```

```
# Create a sample DataFrame
data = {
    'age': [25, 30, 35, 40, 45, 50, 25, 30, 35, 60, 65],
    'income': [50000, 60000, 70000, 80000, 90000, 100000,
55000, 65000, 75000, 110000, 120000]
}
df = pd.DataFrame(data)

# Get descriptive statistics
print(df.describe())
```

This code will provide a statistical summary that includes count, mean, standard deviation, minimum, maximum, and percentiles, helping to understand the distribution of each variable.

Data Visualization

Data visualization is a powerful tool in the EDA process, as visuals can communicate information that is difficult to express in numbers. Below are some useful visualizations.

Histograms

Histograms are an excellent way to observe the distribution of a single variable. They allow you to visualize how many data points fall within certain ranges.

```
import matplotlib.pyplot as plt

# Create a histogram of age
plt.hist(df['age'], bins=5, color='skyblue', edgecolor=
```

```
    'black')
plt.title('Age Distribution')
plt.xlabel('Age')
plt.ylabel('Frequency')
plt.show()
```

Scatter Plots

Scatter plots are useful for observing the relationship between two variables. They allow you to visualize correlations and detect patterns.

```
# Create a scatter plot between age and income
plt.scatter(df['age'], df['income'], color='orange')
plt.title('Scatter Plot: Age vs Income')
plt.xlabel('Age')
plt.ylabel('Income')
plt.show()
```

Boxplots

Boxplots are useful for identifying outliers and understanding the distribution of the data. They show the median, quartiles, and outlier values.

```
# Create a box plot for income
plt.boxplot(df['income'])
plt.title('Box Plot: Income')
plt.ylabel('Income')
plt.show()
```

Tools for Data Exploration

Pandas

Pandas is one of the most powerful libraries in Python for data manipulation and analysis. Its ability to handle data structures like DataFrames and its extensive function set make it an essential tool.

Data Manipulation with Pandas

You can perform various operations with Pandas, such as filtering, sorting, and grouping data. For example, to group data by age and calculate the mean income:

```
# Group by age and calculate the mean income
mean_income_by_age = df.groupby('age')['income'].mean()
print(mean_income_by_age)
```

NumPy

NumPy is another fundamental library for data analysis in Python. Its ability to work with arrays and fast operations allows for efficient computation of complex calculations.

NumPy Operations

With NumPy, you can calculate basic statistics more efficiently compared to traditional data structures.

```
import numpy as np

# Calculate the mean and standard deviation of income
mean_income = np.mean(df['income'])
std_income = np.std(df['income'])

print(f'Mean income: {mean_income}')
print(f'Standard deviation of income: {std_income}')
```

Complete Example of Data Exploration

Below, we present a practical exercise that combines the EDA techniques discussed earlier. Consider a scenario with a dataset about student performance in a class.

```
# Create a sample DataFrame
data = {
    'student': ['Juan', 'Ana', 'Luis', 'María', 'Pedro',
'Laura', 'Antonio'],
    'grade': [65, 78, 82, 90, 55, 62, 85],
    'study_hours': [2, 4, 3, 5, 1, 2, 3]
}
df_students = pd.DataFrame(data)

# Descriptive summary
print(df_students.describe())

# Histogram of grades
plt.hist(df_students['grade'], bins=5, color='lightgreen',
 edgecolor='black')
```

```
plt.title('Grade Distribution')
plt.xlabel('Grades')
plt.ylabel('Frequency')
plt.show()

# Scatter plot between study hours and grades
plt.scatter(df_students['study_hours'], df_students['grade'], color='blue')
plt.title('Scatter Plot: Study Hours vs Grades')
plt.xlabel('Study Hours')
plt.ylabel('Grades')
plt.show()

# Box plot for grades
plt.boxplot(df_students['grade'])
plt.title('Box Plot: Grades')
plt.ylabel('Grades')
plt.show()
```

In this example, we started by creating a dataset that represents students, their grades, and the hours they studied. We then performed several visualizations to explore the distribution of grades and observe the relationship between study hours and obtained grades.

Data Consistency and Cleaning

During data exploration, you may encounter errors or inconsistencies in the dataset. For example, there may be values that fall outside an expected range, duplicate records, or missing values. It is essential to address these issues before proceeding to modeling.

Identifying Duplicates

Duplicates can distort the analysis and are a common error in datasets. In Pandas, you can easily identify and remove them:

```
# Remove duplicates
df_students = df_students.drop_duplicates()
```

Handling Missing Values

Like duplicates, missing values can lead to erroneous analysis. It is important to decide how to handle them: it may be useful to impute, delete, or leave them as they are, depending on the situation. For example:

```
# Impute missing values with the mean
df_students['grade'].fillna(df_students['grade'].mean(),
    inplace=True)
```

Conclusions

Data exploration and analysis are vital steps that lay the groundwork for building effective machine learning models. Through EDA techniques, visualization, and tools like Pandas and NumPy, data scientists can uncover patterns and relationships in the data, a process that improves the quality and relevance of subsequent analysis. As you continue to delve deeper into the field of machine learning, never underestimate the importance of careful data exploration: data that is not understood becomes the models that are not utilized.

www.ingramcontent.com/pod-product-compliance
Lightning Source LLC
LaVergne TN
LVHW051331050326
832903LV00031B/3470
9798315371489